Barney's to Blame

A collection of recent poems

Ross Middleton

Copyright © 2023 (Ross Middleton)
All rights reserved worldwide.

No part of this publication may be reproduced or transmitted in any form or by any means, electronic or mechanical, including photocopy, recording, or any information storage and retrieval system, without permission in writing from the author.

Publisher: Inspiring Publishers,
P.O. Box 159, Calwell, ACT Australia 2905
Email: publishaspg@gmail.com
http://www.inspiringpublishers.com

A catalogue record for this book is available from the National Library of Australia

National Library of Australia The Prepublication Data Service

Author: Ross Middleton
Title: Barney's to Blame
Genre: Fiction, Poetry
Print ISBN: 978-1-922920-16-4

Dedication

To Barney and Lillian Cooney
Good friends and neighbours for years

They are no longer with us
Yet both still live in our minds

(Following there is a short piece indicating Barney's part
In encouraging me to start writing again
Eventually I did
So he must take some responsibility
For some of the words I let loose into the world)

Barney's to Blame

We came to Elsternwick in 2002
For 4 years I settled into the neighbourhood
Got a feel for it
Became a fixture
(In my mind)
Assumed a little responsibility in the local Party Branch
Barney was a politician
We became good friends
Had interesting conversations
Many heartfelt
He did say quietly on occasions
You should write
It echoed a little
Once I had
But not for many years
One day I put pen to paper
In small notepads
Lists of thoughts
Of things to do
Perhaps I was stating to myself
The commitments I'd avoided
One night I filled a notebook
There seemed to be some shape
To what I was saying
A long rambling poem was developing
Rushing somewhere
I was up late that night
Little sleep
Alannah became disturbed
At what I was doing
It seemed important to me
Over the next little while

We had some harsh words
Snapped and bit at each other
The outcome was for me
A short spell in a clinic
For Alannah more disturbance

I could not wait to leave the clinic
And became calm and patient so I could
On release I was more restrained
Eventually I settled
Now I write
Usually late at night
Of what use it is
I'm not sure
It's necessary now
At least for a time

It hurts nobody

Contents

A Beautiful Mind 1
A brief word 4
A Collection 5
A moment in our lives 8
A pleasant Australia Day 2022 10
A repudiation 14
A short list of necessary matters 16
A Statement 19
A visit to the Doctor 22
A word for Kevin 27
An (Un)Certain Presentation 29
An observation of something that can become a serious matter ... 33
An old man's lament 35
Are we nearing the end? 37
Are we secure here in Elsternwick? 40
Butterfly effect 43
Chaos and Order 47
Concocted or false mythology and folk-lore 51
Consider the New World 55
Difficult times in the early 70's 60
Do you know of Tiresias? 65
General rules 68
Getting older 70
History over time 73
How do we say it? 80
How measured should a conversation be? 84
How the West lost? 86
How we decipher situations 92
I will say something simple 95
In Australia's interest? 98

Involvement	102
Keep it brief	106
Law and Morality	109
Linear logic	111
Look both ways	113
Meaning alongside purpose	115
Menzies years ago spoke of the Forgotten People	117
More unfortunate days!	118
Need we always be refined?	121
Not cranky but…	125
Of essential importance	129
One among many	130
Outside or in: where do thoughts come from?	132
Pardon me	134
People should know	136
Polyglot?	139
Rip Van Winkle	144
So!	148
Some say cats have 9 lives	150
Some words	153
Speak up	154
St Kilda	155
Strangers in the house	157
Stress	160
Talk of Dad again	165
The Categorical Imperative	168
The Prime Minister's commitment	170
The shifting world	173
The small and the large	178
The spirit that unites us all?	185
The use of language	189
There must be an explanation	191
Those in control?	195

To generalize	198
To start I could say	200
Today I have to say	204
US Presidents speak	206
Val and me	209
We are mortal	212
We should be patient with those we talk to	213
What do politicians do?	216
What happened and why?	220
What is our country worth?	221
What's happening all over the world?	224
When do we know if it is so?	227
When I am myself and when not	231
Where to start?	235
Why oh why?	241
40 Minutes	244
1979 again	248

A Beautiful Mind

Alannah and I ate out with Les the night before last
Libby joined us after the meal
It was at a Vietnamese restaurant in St Kilda just around the corner
From Chaucer Street and the Peanut Farm
Where I lived for about 6 years over 65 years ago

It was great to see Les and Libby
We had not seen each other for 2 years or more
Libby is a little vague these days
Over the time I've known her I've always considered her
Sensitive cultured and kind
And Lans and I were pleased she came along later

This is not the major reason for my writing
Sometimes I need to ask myself if there is ever a major reason
Yet I need
At least I feel the need to say some things
And at times they come to the fore

Last night I watched A Beautiful Mind starring Russell Crowe
Amongst others
Why?
I knew I'd seen it some years ago
But could not properly remember
So I watched
And I realized

Though the main person involved is not me
There is a sense of identification with him
Yet at the same time major points of difference
He
John Nash is a brilliant mathematician

And generally asocial
Odd let us say
Not having a fully-fledged ability to relate to others
He is absorbed
Or obsessed in his equations

Now despite the fact that years ago
I had some ability in Maths
This is not what stuck in my mind this time
Instead it was the recognition
The discovery once again of his mental illness
And that was more than sufficient for my dismay

His life was not easy
Though finally in 1994 he won the Nobel Memorial Prize
In Economics
He had been recognized

I feel little conviction that I would ever win a Nobel Prize
Nor do I believe I would want to

Yet in the film I see a person
With whom I sympathize
Whose mind in some way is disturbed
And though brilliant in some areas
Not entirely adequate to living a normal life

In a way
Though I am not sure of this
It seems his unbalanced behaviour comes about
Around the time of his entering Princeton University
Something is expected of him
And he expects something of himself

The University
A place where there are minds competing
Does in some way lead to his instability

*

I will leave him at Princeton for a while
And I will leave off thinking and relating for the moment
Though it need be said
The treatment for what is seen as his illness
Had a relation to mine

As you know I am not he
I am me
And he is he
And he is dead by now
But common experiences presented on screen
Leave you thinking

A brief word

It is the year 2022
I am 75 years of age

Between now and my death
I would like to see humanity recognizing
Quite a lot more about what life is

A Collection

The other night I wrote of my rather large collection
Which I have scattered throughout the house
Some in my room
Some in my filing cabinet
And some 70 or so poems in the only book I've ever produced

Talking of my collection
And considering what it covers
I feel now I may have been a little remiss
In fact more than that

I often allow my critical faculty free rein
Not with nasty intent
But using it to express my preference for some matters
Over others

What may be missing?
It's difficult to say properly
But it's possible I have not fully acknowledged humanity's heritage
In many different fields

Sensibly we are aware we are here
Hopefully as some say
On the shoulders of others
Possibly even giants

We certainly need to acknowledge what has gone before
(There will be those kept out of the history books
Forgotten by most
Who considered they hardly mattered)

Yet there are many aspects
Though they are not peculiar to humankind
That can harm others
And there are areas of which we do not think
We can only say
They happened
They're part of our history
And then we're so facile to say
Either it's part of human nature
Or those in the past could not help doing what they did

If people
Scholars or whatever
Argue for the infallibility of past nations
Past human groupings
People of today can easily say
Well what we do should be accepted too
And if we cannot judge right or wrong done in history
Either narrative or particular periods or incidents
We will have little ability to distinguish
The worth of what is done today
Either by us or others
Our words and thoughts will be immune from any ethos

We know we cannot judge all acts
Yet there is the opportunity to choose within reason
If for instance we agree that Western powers over the last
300 years or so
Have exploited native peoples
And forever driven them out
Away from their homelands
From their living
This is something we can say

Yet a student of history is not so restrained
As to only be able to say the above
The lack of validity of royalty and the aristocracy
And of those wealthy and powerful
Come to mind
And we speak out
When we know it's necessary

Yes heritage we have and we need some knowledge of it

But we must not accept only what we're told

We need to know of the inequality and inequity
Throughout
Without simply believing elected leaders
Some are honest some are not
We watch them as well as listening
We accept their job may be difficult
But beware of weasel words
Of false smiles and false acts
Beware of those politicos who believe politics
Is only theatre

And all the electorate needs is a good performance

A moment in our lives

I could well call today and yesterday
Pandemonium for me
Yet I am best to constrain myself
Not allow my blood pressure to rise
Realizing that in fact it should not
For although there was activity
Most was not unpleasant

There are 2 creatures I care for
And I was told yesterday one of them a dog
Whom I love
Though we do not know each other well
Passed away a couple of days ago
I had a very odd reaction
Almost biblical
His human father knocked on our front door
And came down to see me in the lounge room
I was sitting there in a dumbed down fashion
Listening to one of Australia's great batsmen of recent years
Pay tribute to Shane Warne
Australia's and probably the world's greatest spin bowler
Who had died the day before
He was 52 and the country was shocked
And there were many tributes from around the world
I am not able to say he was a brilliant thinker
But I know as a bowler he was
He was exceptional
Working the batsmen out with his skill and application
And more often knowing what was going on
Than the batsman he was attacking
If not subtle in his life
He certainly was at his trade

*

Leave Shane Warne and think of Scooter

When his father Alan came down to see me
He seemed to materialize over my left shoulder
And I said "Peter"
In a few seconds my head fell on my chest
And my arms seemed to be trying to help me with gestures
And almost instantaneously I realized it was Alan
He had kindly come down to tell me of Scooter's passing
I had not dropped in to see them for some while
For fear of hearing this
In my own odd way I tended to believe Scooter was still alive
And with them
And my visiting could only disturb that reality

I would like to write some words for the family
But whatever they would be
It would be hard to uncover
To say the words I felt

He was a Jack Russell
And when I saw him
As I stood with my cane
I could barely stroke the back of his neck

Older
17 and he was not all that well
Yet the family loved him
And I know must already miss him greatly

It may be odd for a man such as I to say
But I do
God bless Scooter
And all who knew him

A pleasant Australia Day 2022

(1)

The day after Australia Day
And the day itself was disturbing
I can't be sure why
But know there was some bad feeling around

A person came by just after my lunch
Was put in front of me
He walked close to my table
I raised my hand to acknowledge him
Just saying Hi
At which point he put his head up slightly
And said Fuck you you fucking bastard
And kept walking past
I did respond
He would have gone 10 to 15 yards past
I said
That's it just stay as a child!

I would in no way believe he wanted a conversation

*

After lunch I took my library book to St Kilda
481 pages of text on Paul Keating
And I considered the reading of it worth my while

I knew the library would not be open
Because of the Public Holiday
And wasn't sure the return chute facility was still available
So I went there

Walking slowly and awkwardly as usual
There was someone sitting up on the steps
Near where the chute was
I asked him if he knew whether it was open
I had a book to return
He said he'd do it for me

I showed him the book as I handed it to him
And said it was on Keating
A politician I had time for
At first in a muttering way he agreed
And said he liked him
Though there was no way I could know
Where this comment came from
It seemed he wanted to talk
And I was prepared to exchange a few words
But the day was over 35 degrees
And it was hot and humid

Then there was introduced some surreality
He wished me Happy Invasion Day
I did start to say something about the inapplicability
Of the word Invasion

If allowed by him there might have been some agreement
For I would call it a takeover
And there is the underlying knowledge of how the British
Saw Australia
But no I had no opportunity at all
As soon as I mentioned I did not call what happened an Invasion
He said I know what you think
Perhaps here I should have asked him how and what
But I didn't
I looked quizzically at him
And started to say what we always need to say

In such situations
Though I said only a few words
The truth is
People have assumptions about others
And instead of either allowing the person to speak
Or at the least testing their own assumptions
What develops is an extremely awkward
And often invalid discussion

The above is fairly true
At least in my mind

What we all need to do is test these assumptions
Not assume them to be true
And do it in a way
That will open up ourselves to others
Our thoughts
And even our prejudices

We must do something to improve the world

(2)

We all have some knowledge of conspiracy theories
And fake news
Generally I try to keep away from the terminology
Attempting to write sensibly and with some truth

So I need to point out another difficulty
We have with language in society
If we allow them to do so there are some words
That come to mind among some people
And it so happens that these words can then
Be adopted by many others
I believe there are quite a number of such words

Though they may have some relationship
To what it is they're describing
The connection is in many cases not well-founded

The outcome can be that in discussion
People talk at odds with each other
Those involved may consider they comprehend the words
And their application
But those in the conversation may be a fair way apart

So today
Whoever we talk to
Or listen to
We need to be more careful with the language

It's often a decisive factor

A repudiation

Emolument – the word comes to mind
As many do
They come and go
There is always movement in the mind
If you allow it
I will agree sometimes
Hopefully not often
It's full of shit
But most activity propagates something
Whatever it might be
There is some choice for us
If we wish geometric patterns
We could design
Or explore those we know
And see them again in a new light

We could of course as some do
Spew forth awful matter
Serious and severe savaging of the world
Yet it is better we know better than this
Have some sense and sensibility
As Jane said years ago
Today's approach would not be the same
Strongly hoping that the class distinctions and disparity
Of all those years ago had gone
Knowing that this does not happen by hope alone
We need to challenge many of the distinctions
Though we use the language
And wish for variety in life
There is much we can't avoid
The strong and full need to be in control
Of our own lives

Nobody should take it from us
Sensible people know this is no cry for absolute freedom
Something only foolish people want
Yet we know we need to resist at times
There are those around us or in authority
Who attempt to compel our thoughts and action
We know most of the rules
And abide by them
But let no-one go too far in their restrictions

We can at times work to a rhythm
Or compose to one
Yet it also should not be constrained within a particular medium
Rap is rap
It does not resonate with me
So it's a path I do not tread

There is a similarity in much of it
There is continuity true
But little or no pause
Something we need at times
For you me and the people around

A short list of necessary matters

(1)

Should I do it or should you?
We could if we were together talking
Conceive the thought and pursue it to some degree
Without fully exhausting possibilities

We would need to remember many
Which are background thoughts
(Or seemingly so)
Form and placement
There needs to be somewhere in us
A meaning
Or hope for it
A sustaining thought or thoughts
We need not follow the religions
Or ideas of perfection or ideal form
(Some things we know are not so)
Yet we need
However high we'd like to soar
To have our feet planted firmly
Here on Earth
As well as knowing we are part of all others here
Though not always fully articulated
They would all make our list

Yet I must warn you
My list does not include the Hitlers and their like
The dictators and tyrants
Those with large egos who believe they have the right
When they're ready
And when they wish
To determine our lives

Not all Titans are destructive
Yet when their belief in themselves over-rides all else
We must speak out and resist

(2)

We all need an outlet of sorts
Some believe sex plays a role
I am too old to contemplate the thought
Too far removed
No longer young I do what I want to do
And what Freud and his ilk have called libido
I divert to other purposes
And have some satisfaction there

(It would help if others followed me a little
Humanity is over-running the planet)
We take over the animal habitats
Many ecosystems are under threat or ruined
We are squeezing the planet dry
All life is threatened
We are the great destroyers

We must recognize that our relationships
Are not only with other human beings
But with all around us

Some will turn to meditation
Eastern or adapted to Western thought
Yet we do not need to do so
Unless it eases us
We know we need rest and sleep
We know we need to pause and think
Life is not all merriment

Things keep happening
We need to be aware
And if we do not see somebody today
We may tomorrow

*

You may be tired of reading me

I will give you one last word of advice
Extend the list in your own way
But remember to keep the ugly thoughts away
If possible

A Statement

Salman Rushdie has been attacked
Badly
I will not tell you of his injuries

It should not have happened

If it was the result of some fatwa or other
We must condemn the fact of them

What is the basis for them?
I do not really know
Yet one major point seems to be if the prophet
Or the religion he espouses is taken in a way
That is considered by his followers to be wrong
Such a fatwa can be issued
And it seems some adherents of the religion
Accept its legitimacy

Given this
In the issuing of the fatwa
There seems to be an acceptance
By the followers
That they can kill or maim those
Who speak against their religion

It is possible we could play it safe now
And agree not to comment on the religions of others
Yet this case matters

I have never been a fan of Salman Rushdie's writing
But he uses his pen to make his point
So we should let him

We should let him without the threat of death
Hanging over him

*

The world is in a very bad place
If people in it have to accept the dictates of religions
If it is assumed that people
Should follow only what are called holy books
Or the words of prophets
And are not able to think for themselves
Or speak and write what they think

It is hardly wise to use vitriol
None of us should
(Though some do)
A sensible approach is best
Yet there is much in religion
All the religions over the world
That many disagree with
There are those who do not believe in any supreme being
Or the words of the prophets

Should those who do
Have the right to tell others
That theirs is the way
Even perhaps the only way?

Such foolishness!

*

The pen and the sword

We would like to believe
(Even let me say as an article of faith)
That the pen will eventually win over the blade in the hand
Yet how often are good words rejected
How often forgotten
And the person with the gun or blade in hand
Cuts short the reasoning that goes on in the world?

It is true
This we know
How slow the words can be
In their influence
In their determination
In their convincing those around

It is a long battle
The words may lose
No matter what they say
How inspiring or heartfelt
The weapons may destroy
Chop off hands or heads
And we remain in a sorry state

Yet give at least some credence
To the written word
The hope is the minds behind these words
May one day prove
If not stronger
At least more durable
Than the muscles of the militants

A visit to the Doctor

(1)

I do not know how the Aboriginal talk of Truth-telling
Came about
Perhaps I will try to find out
However I would not consider it only their way of seeing things
Something their hearts desire
For I too have more than a general regard for truth
So I tell it when I can

To get to it may not always be simple
But at times the path clears
And you find the way

This early morning I realized as I could not sleep
That I was thinking of my having gone to the Blood Unit at
Cabrini Hospital
And seeing Doctor Kirsten Herbert
That in conversation I said to her
As I have said to many doctors over the years
That my Dad wanted the 3 of his sons to do medicine
And by age 15
Though after having had some belief I did
I realized there was indoctrination from Dad involved
I knew I had followed some things beyond his precepts
And certainly not in relation to any vocation

So what I have said to doctors over the years
Is that I never really wanted to do medicine
With the codicil that when the time came to commit myself
I realized I had little interest in the body

This may seem strange
Yet I was then as I am now
Me
Interested in what I'm interested in
Deciding for myself and thinking for myself
Though I followed the teachers in the different disciplines in class
I often thought outside them
Or even (dare I say)? beyond them

And it was the world beyond me that interested me
The thoughts of others
The conversations I had with a wide range of friends
And in a way
The possibilities beyond the body

This does not mean I had no physical aptitude
But my involvement was with what went on around me at the time
As well as in the past
How things came to be
And what they could be
Were somehow of greater importance

So there was the world around me
Local and far away
The thoughts of literature surrounded me
And possibilities abounded

Though culture was not prevalent in the conversation
Of many I knew
I understand now it was a major attraction
A feeling for
An attempt to understand and be part
As well as thinking then what it meant to be where I was
Here in Australia
What it meant to any of us

And it may have been some early thought of identity
But I asked what and why we were here
And not there
Over there
Where many others came from

I had a desire to understand

(2)

There is further background to all this
And it was some attempt to know
God was to be considered
And at times thought revolved around creation
Though I acknowledged to myself
It was more than difficult to place any god anywhere
Other than in the many stories told

Beyond us and around us there was space and time
Not background as some might think
But always close to mind

Philosophy and thoughts of the Cosmos mattered to me

I think it foolish for parents to always treat their children
As children
I have noted many parents who do not recognize
A maturity in the youth

What is learnt in family and among friends
As well as in the classroom
Should be only the beginning of understanding
And knowledge of the world
Small increments or large
They happen over time

Outside the expected pathways
And youth can take advantage of them
Responding with real curiosity to all around

So I do not wish to damn my father
In many ways he was a good and moral man
Though unfortunately in his work situation
From early on he had pretty much to fend for himself

And he wanted us his 3 sons
To have the advantages
He did not have

By the time I turned 15
I was aware
When Dad and I confronted each other
There had been divergence between us
A divergence not evident
For at least quite a few years
With the 2 other sons

So I was the one to bear the brunt of his blast
I would not demean him with the word bombast
But he argued in the vein he must have at work
A strong unionist with strong views
Whatever the subject he had to know he was in the right

And that is a large part of what was wrong
Our argument could have been a decent conversation
Civil and of some restraint
But no
When the blast of war sounds in your ears
The answer is to smite the foe
And in my not agreeing with him
I had to be brought under control
In other words defeated

These last words I did not say to Dr Herbert
But at times there is a need to understand
What is important in any situation
And never more so than when talking about
Parents and their children

As I say
I told Kirsten only the first part of this piece
I've now almost finished

But I did feel comfortable with her as a person
And considered her more than competent in her role
She was able to listen and could explain to me
The medical situation

*

I am a person who is hardly able to dissemble
I usually say what I feel
And so I did on the day I saw Dr Kirsten Herbert

As we parted I said to her
It's been a pleasure to meet you

A word for Kevin

The truth is I'm too old and tired
To say anything profound
Words of wisdom do not drop from my mouth

I still think quite a lot
Yet most of the time I am a good-natured person
And tend to avoid hard argument
Rather positioning myself at some distance
For the sake of my sanity
Something I need intact

There are times that I may enter the discourse
Thoughts flow
Words too
And names and concepts involved in whatever it may be
But I need to be fairly relaxed

My history is fairly good
And having made some attempt to understand what it is I am
The story of my life
If told in part
Can be interesting

I have causes
Quite a few
But cannot these days follow all of them
Whether for good or bad
Success or not
Leave it to the young
Those more engaged

Lacking physical activity
In fact having what I would call these days
A failed body
I am not complete
Though it is not possible to isolate your own awareness
To know where it comes from and how you use it
The body is an important part of it
So become older
And in many ways your awareness fails too

However remember this about anyone
There can be the right moment
Or the right encounter
The one that stimulates
And can hold you in its thrall
For some time

Always remember Socrates
Know thyself
(Though not excessively)
And work outwards from there

It can be surprising how far you can go

An (Un)Certain Presentation

We must not sell ourselves
Or be slaves to others
We need some idea of self
But need not advertise it fully or forever

We can ask what we should present
And lay out some matters that are integral to us
We would start with birth and family
Nuclear or extended
As well as friends at school
Those of our youth
Those of our neighbourhood
And acknowledge those many we have known over years

*

Spontaneity
Perhaps that is one answer
If you know yourself you can speak to others
Without invasion or transgression

Yet today I have another answer to what to do
Many may not like it
Many may not agree
And may never do it

*

There can be uncertainty in many of the thoughts we have
Yet we write them down
Fix them on paper or computer
And there comes some form of certainty
A shape that expresses what you want to say

At times you need to stop and think
Finding yourself to be over-confident
And perhaps even over-bearing

Yet with reflection on past thoughts
And with the continuity of many of them
There may eventually be a certainty in your life

*

I do not like arguments
Yet sometimes find myself involved

I have an answer to others
One not entirely applicable
Nor easily presented to all

It may seem that in your presentation
You are avoiding the opinions of others
Yet no
You have your work
Having written on many subjects
Over a fairly wide range
You can talk of this presentation to others
It is your own collection
Your attempt to understand the world
And things in it
As well as what we can of the stars above
In their formation
Their clusters
And relation to the Universe

*

I have done one book
Fairly simple
But now I have in total almost 1800 poems
They are my Collection
They are neither love poetry nor lyrical
I do not stress metaphor
Though using it occasionally
Often I try only to state what is

Whatever the case it's my truth
I may fail in insight or perception true
But at least have made an attempt
To relate to others what I think
The question of belief is in ways another matter
But thought and belief have some relationship

Or so I believe

*

So what is the final word?

Fairly simply
With all the disagreement in the world
All the argument
And often anger
It helps to have a Collection
Of what I hope are in some way good words
To occasionally print
In place of what may go on
At times when people get together
Sometimes pain and anger
Causing dissension among them

*

So I show my work around at times
It may help
It may heal
It may indicate progress a little above the purely material sense

An observation of something that can become a serious matter

Well I listen to and watch economists too
Not only detailed documentaries
But one such as a webinar I watched tonight
It was Richard Denniss the Chief Economist at the Australia Institute
Interviewed by Alex Sloan
Who is I believe also involved there

They were in front of an audience
And it was a way of presenting Dr Denniss' latest book
A copy of which I have
Though as yet unread

Looking back about 4 years ago I had bought his book on neoliberalism
Read it and then lent it to someone
Who eventually lost it
So recently I borrowed it from the St Kilda Library
And have almost finished it again

He's quite stimulating in his presentation
Obviously an ongoing thinker
And covers most of the questions of the Australian economy
His work reminds me to some extent of that of Ted Wheelwright
Who was a Political Economist of some years ago
A person I referred to often

*

Question time came
And I was almost going to turn the webinar off
And do other things
But I listened with some interest to the first question

I could not catch the words well
But something struck me about them
The question was phrased in a general way
Asking Can we…?
Probably the public the electorate or those members of the audience
As I said
I could not catch the words clearly
Yet it disturbed me as questions often do in these situations

Do not damn the expert unless you disagree seriously
With him or her
But can't the question be put more directly by the person asking it?
By her expressing it in a way
That indicates she has a sense of the answer
And strength in her question
There are situations in which we should not disregard statements
Of this kind

Could it not be asked
If Dr Denniss were to agree with the proposition put forward
And in this way allow the questioner some agency
In her question
As well as understanding the possibilities potentially there
In the words she used?

*

This is not an attempt to attack an expert
Nor to break down the edifice of his thought
Yet somehow on these occasions there should be an opportunity
For the listener to participate in some way
And not be solely resigned to a passive role

An old man's lament

Here again sitting and waiting and watching
Though there is no desperation around me
I have my pen and notebook
I am of an age and have some experience
A certain knowledge too
Which has taught me what to do
And how to cope
Within the surroundings to which I'm limited

The waiting is no great chore
Every day I sit here
And things happen
I greet the dogs and the people
All different shapes and sizes
As well as colours
At times groups small or large
Will stop and talk
And sometimes we engage further
There should be if possible
No forced response or emotion
Leave yourself as open as you can to the world

And then let it be
Something we learn over time
Maturity development little matter what you call it
You live a while on this earth
And if you have learnt little
You fail yourself
As well as those around
We all need insight into ourselves
And our surroundings
If we have sense and some learning

We might use the word environment
Or eco-system or habitat
And pay attention to animals
Other than those some call pets

There is a mix of people walking by
As well as dogs
Big small and individual
Some young some old
And there is a mix between the people and the animals
Ranging over all ages
As well as their response and affection

We do not want presumption on the part of people
Those advertising themselves
And their achievements

There should be no pass or fail
Distraction can be good
But it can also be dubious
Who is to say?
Who is to judge?

What we want is good people going by
Though the parade will not always satisfy
We continue to watch
Until we die

Are we nearing the end?

As a person who attempts to range widely
Over different subject matters
There at times come difficulties
That anyone could foresee

In the past
Some fair while ago now I experienced psychiatric difficulties
And spent time in mental hospitals
Yet this is time ago
And though I am aware of the danger of stretching too far
I do not fear it now
At this present moment

While the above is true I know
That there is some sort of build-up around me
Of matters I feel I need to deal with
There are some I have
As well as others I have made rather patchy starts on

Autobiography history
And thoughts about the world and the countries there
Especially at this time the war between Ukraine and Russia
I cannot resolve any of these matters personally
Certainly not in my own head
But as in many things an approach is needed
I can't be satisfied unless I think on it
And lay out the problems involved
In a way that gives me some grip on them

*

The above is part of all the happenings around

At the moment here in Australia
We are in the last few weeks before a Federal election
Something else that occupies my mind
Though I do not participate in the activity these days
Age has taken its toll
And in some ways
Through necessity
I stand apart

Briefly however there are issues that are important
One is the Uluru Statement to the Heart
The Indigenous words to all of us
Voice Treaty and Truth-telling
All necessary
Yet they will not come about easily

I leave this comment here
My sympathies are with the people
Though I cannot travel or engage fully with them

For me Social Media is no answer
So I can only write and talk
And hope my words get around somehow

We do not need to ask:
How unsettled is this world of ours?
The planet we live on
Is subject to global warming
There is no doubt
And I for one
And I among many
Feel not enough has been done
There is activity

But here in Australia our leaders have trapped us
In a cycle of oil gas and coal
The money nexus is a serious part of our problem
Covid has contributed to difficulties in coping
But it should in no way be used as an excuse
For the failings of people and the government

The warming
I might once have said
Is background to our troubles
Yet using the word background is hardly sufficient
The truth is continually confronting us
The whole world is unsettled
Today in many ways in many places
Climate is unknowable
Yet we see and hear of its devastation at times
Surely enough to keep it in our mind's eye

*

I do not pray
Today I can only appeal to those who care
To those young old and middle-aged
Who can do something about the impending situation

The thought of humans being the Guardians of the Planet
Must mean something

Let us live up to the thought!

Are we secure here in Elsternwick?

I sit inside the café on my own
I'm happy enough here
I know people
And the staff are wonderful
Very nice to me
And at the same time efficient

From my corner I look out
The day is warm
20 degrees or more
My shirtsleeves are rolled up
I like it that way
So when I go out I'll feel the breeze on my arms

Looking out I am taken in to some extent
By watching a few people sitting at the tables
On the sidewalk
They are talking
Some of them at length
I'm not wondering what
But they are talking
And I know there are more words being released
Into the world
At least our area
Our suburb

We know something of what goes on here
But by no means all
Things change over time
As we all know
And need to remind ourselves

There are opposite rather tall buildings
Housing apartments or flats
Whatever the word may be
And this
The main street in Elsternwick
Is being overhung more and more
And it is not only in Main Street
Much has changed around the area

There are many questions surrounding these facts
Population growth
More children
Crowding
Housing
And the nature of the area has changed considerably
Since we came here 20 years ago

(At that time I would call Elsternwick a village
Though the term was a little fanciful
It had some truth in it)

*

I said the above to James
A 22 year old student in History and Literature at Monash
He works at Vintage Cellars
Where I buy my beer
Light beer these days
Oldie that I am
And James responded saying how his parents said something similar
To my thoughts
The place has changed

We know we need to be political at times
We know we need to be aware
And what many of us don't want
Is for developers to take over the area
To exploit it
To exploit us
Though they tell us it's for the good of the place
While we know there is a major thought involved
The fattening of their pockets

And we know they can do this
Through select lobbying
By using funds to influence politics at all levels

Butterfly effect

How did I find a title for this?
I borrowed it from the show I watched tonight
I've seen 7 out of 8 half hour episodes
They're not hopeless
Yet there is no doubt there is a form of indoctrination in them

Can they be excused?
Well it's necessary to understand what they're doing
What they're presenting
And the questions they're not asking

*

We know of the butterfly effect
By no means a fully blown theory
Just an idea indicating how a happening somewhere
Can change the environment
Having an effect on happenings elsewhere

If taken to an extreme this view may allow
Great changes over space and time

There is an unpredictability about many events
Though we humans attempt to understand
And sometimes contain or control

I believe most people would not consider this response
As going too far
If there are dangerous consequences that may arise
From this flutter of the wings
It's best to be prepared
And if precaution is necessary take it

*

Now this 8th episode of the program
Dealt with the development of the Internet
An interesting résumé
And neat

There was a sentence in the middle of the show
Something to the effect
That it is not possible to know
What the future of any invention will be
Yet we need to give them a go

You can see where this leads
It is in its own way a comment on creativity and development
And human development generally

*

Let's say we leave the sentence sitting there in the middle
Give it a go!
I am not one to say no
Yet what we do needs thought
Not just creative ability
Or entrepreneurship

*

I invite you to the end of the program
The voice from the TV
Tells us the Internet provides freedom
It also changes our lives
Instead of living in and relating mainly to the family group
The whole world is open through the Internet

And it also mentions that people can then be individuals
A contention I find to be strange

And loaded in the favour of the voice
Sensibly we are all individuals
Yet in this contention of the Net's potential
It would be providing something more
Are we at this stage to say subtly?
Or should we use the word blatantly?
Though there is community involvement on the Net
There is a strong sense of something I cannot condone
That is
The Philosophy of Individualism

We will all be apart from others at times
Yet pursue the thought of individuality too rabidly
And there is danger there
Too great thoughts of your own self
Paranoia too
Which can lead you not to people
But away

*

Two final matters

One is the seemingly American nature of the program
In the last couple of minutes or so
China and its restrictions are mentioned
The producers of the program have an agenda
As do many other people

Secondly
The way the figure directing the thoughts presented
Talking about history and the way it might go
Claiming there are turning points in history
Is simplistic
It's like a form of wish fulfilment

Though physical happenings may be affected
By the flutter of the butterfly's wing
It is a poor way to look at history
Any counterfactual attempts to explain historical events
May have some interest
But hardly any of them can fully encompass
The changes that in fact may be said to occur

The program
Though at least grounded in this last episode
Is very like fiction

[And to emphasize:
We know if we have a thought or conceive of a worthwhile invention
We should at the very least consider its future consequences

We need to at this point disregard
The willing suspension of disbelief]!

Chaos and Order

It is not certain whether we are talking about human beings
Or nature or the stars in the sky
Or the Universe itself

Yet to narrow it down a little
Let's talk of a young child
Really a baby born
Dependent on its mother
It whatever gender could easily be seen as chaotic in response
If
And this is a big If
Its mother did not attempt and in many ways train the child
To respond in certain ways
In fact to organize the child's life from the beginning
A child needing support of course
As all do
Yet the amount given will differ from parent to parent

So is the orderliness that the child displays
Inherent or genetically determined
Or is it something less than that
Though order is still important
As it is imparted

To what degree does the child
Either at first the baby
And then the growing creature
Have apart from its learnt behaviour
An inherent restlessness or even chaotic spirit?

Would we look to the Cosmos here
To see the swirling gas and the final formation of stars

Which eventually destroy themselves
Creating a cycle of birth and rebirth?

How close are we to the Universe?
Are we part?
Does the surrounding reality somehow determine us?

We cannot here look to Astrology for an answer
It is archaic and largely set
Our minds over time have grown beyond the early thoughts
The child grows
The adult develops further

Yet we fit somehow

Even if it is only to see ourselves
Against the backdrop of the Universe

*

Let us leave the questions of children and the Universe
And give an indication (only that)
Of why I might be considering chaos and order

There is an essential reason arising from Alannah
Saying quite frequently I am chaos
With the implication that she is the opposite
A person embodying order

There is some truth in this
Though I will not go fully into the depths of the reality
Around us
Family upbringing yes
And also the fact that Alannah was a reference librarian
At the State Library for 38 years

Obviously she had a need for order
Or in that job her existence would be threatened

I have had different work experiences
Labouring taxi driving factory work
As well as the Public Service and teaching

One would expect that a primary school teacher
Should be orderly in approach
There is truth in that
But I did not overdo the order
Or apply strict borders to learning
Curiosity was important
And as far as possible my job was
To stimulate creativity among the children
In Maths English and any drama I was involved in
I also took the boys for sport
So there was a loose and friendly relationship

Would anyone call this chaos?
I doubt it

Let us turn towards this creature some call chaotic
Be it god or man (or woman)

Whatever those of orderly mind may believe
The creature is not forever in one state
It changes
And there is movement
Whatever it might be
There is movement through time and space

Is it necessary to time this movement
Or stipulate the place it might be at a particular time
Or is the movement a creative act in itself?

Must we accept the definitions of some
That chaos incarnate cannot really be so
Because it cannot express what it needs to
When necessary

*

Typification is troublesome
Accept other people's
And you will be locked in by their thoughts

In any relationship you will have different qualities
Varying qualities
Some are good and even admirable
Some perhaps less so

All sensible people need to understand
That in this world they must at times judge situations
And even other people
If the others do real harm your judgement may be harsh
But if they don't it's best to view the situation flexibly
Being as open as you can
And not destroy the possibilities of affection between people

Concocted or false mythology and folk-lore

Many of us at one time or another
Talk of myths and legends
There are some we accept
Some we do not
At least in their entirety

We do know that many people use language quite loosely
And it would be fair to say
The ideas surrounding these myths and legends
Might be more than fluid
They may often be extremely difficult to pin down
In any satisfactory way

Most of us would believe that there are many aspects of these stories
From the past
However long ago
Or even for that matter fairly recently
That would be exaggerated in ways by some groups
Many who might hardly have regard to the truth
That could possibly be contained
In fact those perpetrating the stories
Have their own reasons for doing so
Sometimes consciously
Sometimes not so much
But they do so with a desire
To perpetuate thoughts for reasons which they believe to be so

In all this there can be the passing down
Of what are considered to be truths
But may have essentially little basis

In different societies we can isolate these stories
And without calling them lies
We can see how they fail any test we may ask of them
Any proper substantiation of their validity

This can be a serious worry in a society
It can be a serious worry in the minds of people
If they once attempt to clear them

An interjection is needed here
Every society needs a form of functioning reality
If thinking people entirely cut away any basis the group has
There can be serious disturbance
Yet in a good society nothing is more needed
Than a proper and at times rigorous dialectic

The world today is likely to go through harsh times
But even with the attempt to sustain our bonds
We need to continue to question them

There is no doubt some see continual questioning
As a tedious exercise
It should not be seen in this way
It is not an exercise in which we flex our muscles
It is part of the mental stimulus we need to keep going
Even when times are hard

Question ourselves at times
And question what is going on around
If the world keeps going as it is
We are challenged greatly
Many of the living areas and habitats and even edifices
Are changing over time
We know of the change in energy production

As well we need an awareness of changes in living habits
Our eating habits and farming
And food production generally

*

After looking back what is it we think we need to do?
One thing is to as far as possible
Isolate the truths of the past as well as we can
This does not mean a complete rejection of the stories
Or myths or legends
Those that have featured for years
The human imagination is important
It's best not to put it in a corner
At the same time knowledge and understanding
Come over time
And some
If not many of these tales of yesteryear
Are essentially that:
Tales of yesteryear

Not all will want to be close reading
Or detailed in their historical searchings
But all will show sense
If they are careful when generalizing
About matters in the past
That are with little doubt
Uncertain

Here Science matters
History with all the individual disciplines
Archaeology Anthropology physical or social
Palaeontology as well as knowledge of continuing or fluctuating
Environmental factors
Throughout time

Though some may incline towards seeking religious truths
In stories that have been presented to them
I can only suggest the stories themselves
And their bases need to be questioned

Humans went wrong when they turned to God
People conceived of something greater than they were
And then allowed the thought to float there
Above their heads
Way above
As time went by more was attributed to these gods or God
And it took still more time
To realize what had always been necessary:
The questioning

Wind up your thought and all the complications
And call it faith
It's a way out of many arguments
And any sense of reality

Consider the New World

America is a large country well-populated
I'm not sure how we would generalize about its people
Many are proud
Believing they are strong and resourceful
And their country is the greatest in the world
Actually many of them believe they lead the world
And also believe they should
They seem to be a country with some relationship with God
Whatever that might mean
We do know however
That many of their leaders close their speeches
With the refrain God bless America

An Empire they are and strong
In military and industry
It is noticeable that in signing off their officials
Do not bless the world
But we know enough has been written of the USA
For us to be aware of their Exceptionalism
Something if it were to be a fact
Would give them licence to do things
Many countries would not
Or perhaps could not

*

Yet sometimes they must worry

Looking at them over the last few years
We are led to ask
Are they toppling or flailing?
We see so many things going wrong there

Injustice unfair legislation and executive decisions
At times by Presidents
As well as disturbance in the land

I am sure they are not all bad
They help the world in some ways
But when they believe it is their role to direct it
And determine how it should be
We are not only worried
We need to resist
Speaking out against the one-sided nature of
any supposed partnership
They use our country to train their troops
And they use the land to situate surveillance stations
And we go along willingly

So is this what has become of the New World?
In both countries the original inhabitants having little say
Or hold on the land or its wealth?

*

It is 3 days ago that I wrote the above
I'd lost my train of thought
A sad fact

Yet we often need to start again
Let us talk of Australia
Or at least of me
Somehow here we are part of what is called the New World
As is the USA
It is a term that we all might like to believe
Helped us on our way
Made us define ourselves
As distinct from the old countries
Including Europe and its ways

I would like to think we could do things
The older countries failed to do
In a serious field
One in which we relate to one another as equally as possible
Did not only accumulate wealth
But sought some meaning in our lives

A person who talks of meaning is by no means necessarily
Only young in thought
With the attempt
We would expect commerce and trade
Production in certain areas
Though not to excess

*

Religion is in most ways culturally determined
It is not something we want to be ruled by
There is choice in the matter
As well as the knowledge that a person can live a good life
Outside the prevailing religions

We must say at this point
That whatever we aim for
If there is to be success
It must be of humanity itself

There are many foolish thoughts

Most of us produce in some way
And consume
Yet this we do only in a particular role
In a time and place

Some would say production and consumption is not the measure of a man
Or a woman
Or whatever else we might name ourselves

The production cycle can be difficult
Especially for those with little say in it
Little control
Remember Marx wrote of the social relations of production
And it is in the work setting
That they need to be fair

To achieve something approaching an exchange
That can be of some satisfaction to all sides
This fairness must exist
And the thought simple as it is
Is telling

Today it is time for the work situation
To be part of an Industrial Democracy
Where force does not rule
And nobody is a slave

In many areas there are people
Often women
Subject to their superiors

When men can treat them as sexual objects
And see no harm in it
There is a need to call them out

It happens
We know it happens
A society without such exploitation
In the many areas we know it exists

Might well not be quite as rich
As people would believe they wanted

We need to continually ask what it is we're aiming for

It is not possible to accept the disparities in people's situations
The world has hardly progressed
When the above is taken as a measure

How do you tell the whole world to behave?

There is no way at all
There can only be a beginning if you start with your own country

*

At this point we can agree
It's best to leave the problems of the USA for a while
And focus fully with sense
On our own country Australia

Let us keep hope in our hearts
And continue the conversation

[Turn this page and you will find nothing else written]

Difficult times in the early 70's

About 50 years ago I was young
And was still attempting to find my way
Despite my father's interference in many important thoughts I had
I leave this for now
Most I have mentioned over the last few years
As well as lambasting him for his essentially halting any progress
I might have made
3 years Matriculation
2 years at Monash Uni passing only 2 subjects
Being posted for months on the board at the front of the library
Banned for the many books I had borrowed and not returned

At least it was all in some way
In the cause of auto-didacticism
The only option open to me
With my refusal to commit myself
To any formal learning

Then there was an interim
When I was away from my parents' home
By this time they had left the shop
The newsagency
And I did not know this for months
Having no contact with them

Eventually I went back to live with them
And though over the years they did their best
I was never comfortable

At this time I was writing something to do with the aborted children
Between Val and me
I had no way of approaching it directly

Yet as I wrote it was there on my mind
Largely I encompassed it in some way
Not in meaningful disguise
But in the context of my life over the last few years

Mum and Dad and my younger brother Kent
Were all living in the 2 top flats
Of a building we owned in St James' Park Hawthorn
There were difficulties involved for me in all this

I had to smoke in the toilet off my bedroom
And dip the cigarette in the bowl to put it out
And then keep them somewhere
(I don't remember where)
In a bag
Probably it was in my desk
Mum would have smelt them
But she didn't say anything

It was a difficult time
Though not all bad
Next door there were the Diamonds
The mother and her 3 children
The father a psychiatrist had abandoned them
And gone over to the States to race in some form of motor sport
I knew the children needed some form of father figure
But also know you cannot just pick up such a role
However I was friendly with them
And perhaps helped a little emotionally

By this time I had started
Doing a Primary Teaching Diploma at an Independent College
Being too late to apply for the Government one

So I was studying
Though not in the way most people do
As well as writing for myself
It was perhaps to be a short novel
The circumstances of my living around the time I was writing about
Were to me interesting
I would also try to be as honest as I could about them
And all involved
Val Sid John Chris and the 2 Elizabeths
And in doing so attempt to pin down in some way
What I had done over this time
That led me
To be the unfortunate father of 2 children
Dead before birth

This is all a long time ago
And I am not a great one for guilt
But I had involved myself in something
I know I should not have
And I needed to understand
How and why it came about
And how anything of this nature ever does

There was an added difficulty
And it was my mother
I was typing the manuscript (if it could be called that)
And Mum over time looked at it
In the drawers of my desk
She was unhappy about it
And said I should leave it alone
As well as forgetting Val

There is background here
Mum would have loved to have been a writer

She was a prolific reader
Unfortunately she had had very little education
And that only at a primary level

I loved my mother
But I could not answer her
The truth was I was still trapped at home
And if one parent my father
Had caused me such trouble
Mum at this time was not helping me

Trapped yes
With little money
I could not handle the idea of doing more labouring
Either private work factories or in the railways
So I could see no way out

So I stuck at the course
And though I did not complete it
Some good came of it

Yet anyone who does not know me
Should be told:
Dad set me up in an impossible situation
When I was 15
His lack of understanding
Impinged so strongly on mine
And caused me to doubt myself
Beyond belief

It might have worked out
If he had been rational
Yet he could not be
Society had seriously affected him
And determined his views

One could say as my brother Kent has
He was a father
With Kent's implication he was doing his best
Yet I knew when Dad and I disagreed
That I was right
Something I still know
Yet he exerted a force no parent should

Do you know of Tiresias?

Definitions – Bah!

Am I so crude or critical?
Or do I know that though we need to describe the world
As fully as we can
For our own sake
And for communication with others
There lies danger in accepting definitions of things
In an attempt to understand

Is it a claim of belonging to some group of people
With the same defined ability or disability
So you can know who you are
And where you fit?

Sorry to say to people but I must
This is unthinking identification
Yes use the word (the definition) for a while
To understand what it might say of you
But do not believe you are irrevocably tied to it

If the word is useful for your purpose
The understanding of self
Or whatever else you might need
(Sometimes the understanding of others)
Use it
But be in mind
Words like most things wear out over time
They need rest
And so do you
The interpreter

So if the word you find applies to you
Whether welcome or not
Attempt to understand what's behind it
The meaning
The history
And why you (or others) might be said to suffer
(If suffering is what we're talking about)

Over time we gain perspective
Or we should
And if we are to have an integrated self
There are some words and phrases we will need to cast away
And
Recognize that it is not only ourselves
We should attempt to understand
But the world around
And in this world
Labels are not sufficient
In any adequate description of us
Or all around

*

[The above was after a discussion with Lauren on gender
Not my favourite subject
Lauren was presenting herself as an advocate
For those with gender concerns
Not to be unfair, but the thought stirred in my mind
It was possible it concerned her personally more than she said

She said I pointed as I spoke
Yes I do quite often
With shaky hand
Yet it was at least in part a recognition

That the talk was between us
Murray said little
I'm sure he would have thoughts
But did not voice them

Perhaps another time]

General rules

Sometimes I think people think I'm a little odd
When talking over something
Either a political point or a moral matter
I will bring up what I call my General Rule
About a particular aspect of life
It seems fairly obvious to me that most people
Do not see life this way
I do not wish to say others are inadequate
But when in discussion an ad hoc response is discernible
From the other
And you can only wonder

Can it be that I think
That the person I'm talking to has hardly ever considered
The situation we're discussing
Or is it that they've never attempted to clarify their thoughts
On the subject at hand?

A general rule will never cover every aspect
Of any subject you attempt to understand
But at the least it's a good guideline
At times you may not stick to the generality you state
And this can mean a number of things
It can be a transgression
For which you must hold yourself responsible
But it may not be so dire
It might well be an exemption
That does not fit under the umbrella
You've opened over yourself

The umbrella analogy may be a good one
It saves you from a drenching

An exemption might allow you to step over a yawning puddle
Holding your brolly firmly
In a position still able to keep the rain off

*

So I'll leave you here

If you have no interest in general rules
Take no heed of me

But there are different approaches to thinking
Different methods
You may not need a textbook

*

We know we will over time
Hear reasonable thought from others

Getting older

Yes I will soon turn 76 on Anzac Day this year
Only 8 days away
I won't say I can't wait
Actually though I mentioned it in a poem I did
The other day
Without it seeming to matter
Whether it was so or not
I've now thought again
76 is not 75
So I'm not getting younger
And 75 I've quite liked
3 by 25 are good numbers
And though as I wrote elsewhere a week ago
I have no belief in numerology
I have a little feeling about leaving my present age
And going further
76 and it could be said going further into the nether regions
I have no intimations of hell or damnation
Or any Christian-chartered places
It might be that some might believe I'd wait in purgatory
Forever
No
Yet I also would not place myself among others
In Dante's Circles
There are huge fabrications there available to us
If we believe the thoughts they did then
But no I do not

If anything these nether regions must finish somehow
Or somewhere

But I identify with Odysseus
Perhaps next to me
Seeing the shades of the dead appear
After I cross the river Styx

Is this a longing for mythology
Something I still have
Though I often repudiate story-telling or myths
The way they're told and why it is they are

These nether regions are here
The word is meaningful
Am I still these days longing for another time
Wishing for Gods in the sea
Or sprites in streams
Or do I just feel unhappy not being able to travel
I would if I could
I could go anywhere

In Greece I would have familiar feelings
Or go to places I studied in the 80's
A number of Asian countries
If there were spirits there
And I do not say there are
I might get a fuller sense of the world
More full than I allow myself now

If the spirits are not there
It matters little
The experience would surely inspirit me
And that is what I want

Not to be forever locked in this day and age
My mind has always ranged over space and time

Once my body did too
Though less than I would like

And today mind and body are restricted

*

Are we here already:
                        In the nether regions?

History over time

(1)

There is no doubt that what happens in human lives
And society changes over time

There are many aspects we could look at
Too many
So to pick a date or time which did bring significant change
Let us say 1492
And thereafter

It is said once there was the Old World
And then the New
The Americas are significant here
Australia is some part

This view is of course Eurocentric
But let us accept it for the moment

What did we see in these new lands?
(I am not denying others such as those in the Pacific)
Well until America's War of Independence
Or as some call it Revolution
Many of the newcomers were called colonials
Yet with the break with Britain
And the sometime alliance with France
Things changed
It could be said there was a sense of independence
And at the same time opportunity

With the taking over of lands from Spain and Mexico
There was room
They had what Hitler didn't in Europe

What he called lebensraum
And they took it
Many of them went west
Across the plains
Across the Rockies
And they had a sense of space and freedom

Or is this only a story?

They did have some freedom though
Over time they were able to drive the Native Americans
From the East westwards
And finally dispossess them

These people had their culture
Their ways and beliefs
Yet many of the newcomers took little notice
They were seen as an obstacle
Especially by those on the ground
And the government and government officials

Yes the new arrivals established their freedoms
And they were proud people
And they instituted guns in their national mind
A natural weapon
Yours to have and to hold
A shame I would think
The marriage of humanity and an instrument
Of killing efficiency

(2)

We could ask of Australia
Another said to be of the New World
How different were we

Or our forebears
In dealing with Native Australians?
There was contact of course
As there always was in these situations
There was also conflict

Today we can look back and say
The British claimed the country
An Empire believing it had the right
We could call it thoughtless
But that would be excusing them
They did what other newcomers did
Made up things
Were creative in their beliefs
Which were founded on lies

In the Americas there were significant civilizations
For thousands of years
In Australia the people here have inhabited the land
For tens of thousands of years

The original inhabitants of the New World
May never assume the rights they had many years ago
Today they protest for them

(3)

For the time being let us move back to America
And acknowledge how they were creative in many ways
Some of them took money-making to the extreme
This we know
But there was a basis for this
Something illustrated in the violence of the Western movement
The fights the conflict were not only between the newcomers
And the Native Americans

There was a mix between different forms of farming and husbandry
And other possibilities the country offered
We know of the West
The Wild West
Or do we?

Here in Australia we were brought up on films
Westerns mainly during our early years
The guns used
The stoicism of the pioneers
And these films of the time took a stance
In simple terms there was the good and the bad
And from this time away
I can only assume we were to decide which was which

Gore Vidal wrote his series on the American Empire
One of the books is given over to the development of Hollywood
There were many assumptions in the films of early Hollywood
Of course sort them out properly
And you would be a good American
Or even a good Australian

In the age of cinema much was borrowed
So much influenced people's thinking
Most sociologists fail in their evaluation of it
So is the answer they have
A conclusion:
We all have free minds
Floating it might be said
But floating where?

We cannot ignore lessons in stories
Whatever the critics say
Some point a moral

An indication of what is right or wrong
Sometimes it is even laid out as to why

To be entirely sensible
And without reference to what American citizens
Regard as their rights
One important lesson
Was that guns dealt death
They dealt it in the old days
And in the USA they do so today

If this is so
It is possible we could do something about it
Boycott their goods and services
Boycott their influence
As well we may find we may well have to boycott
Their thinkers and politicians

(4)

No I am not doing America a disservice
Yet unfortunately I know they are not alone in what they do
Many countries do wrong too

One could say a major matter was the Civil War
Of great importance in the Nation
However it seems to me to be that division
Is part of their way of seeing things
Division in the Nation
Division from countries other than their own
Those who do not toe the line
And division in themselves

We could say guns and killing came to the fore
During the Civil War

But looking back beyond that
We know there was a history
Some were fur trappers and dealers
Some over time came west homesteading
They came from many countries
And in a way they mixed
Though often they resisted it

Does anyone believe these settlers
Arriving from the Old World
Would form a whole
A nation to be proud of
Or is it more important to have an understanding
Of how they papered over the cracks
Often in the early homes
As well as in the truth about the wrongs many of them did?
Many died at the hands of those arriving
And many justifications were given
What was done had to be made respectable
In some sort of way
And there was a God many turned to for justification

So the words
God bless America
Were supposed to cover all

Sins and incivility and slavery

(5)

So we leave it here
Some among us talk of progress
Is it the tall buildings
The long bridges spanning rivers
And the major Universities

The businesses in competition
The numerous states
Both of mind and spread geographically across the land?

How many lands?
How many countries?

Why do they do it?
Spread themselves across the globe
Are we to believe they have good intentions
In doing what they do
Or does the American ego come so close to bursting
Needing to have a say in everything?
And their say is tantamount to control of all they can

You are either with us or against us
It's an American definition
Hanging in the air it concerns us all

And we know if it's there
It may one day fall

How do we say it?

Religion is the wrong interpretation of the world
Any religion would be

What we would want to discover
I can only assume is something relating to humankind
Yet not caused by it
And almost certainly something that would not assume
That only humankind was involved
There would be as we know
Knowledge surrounding the assumptions
Not necessarily entirely complete
But a history of what humankind has come to understand
As the Universe of which we are all part

Often we need to know
What we do not know
So we work with the possibilities
The answers that others have provided for us
Or those we have found for ourselves
Over the millennia

There will be a time when we will need
To understand the truth
Or significance of what we have learnt

*

Today there is a wide range available to us
Planets stars and galaxies
And all of them galore
The need to reflect on how time plays a part
In our surroundings

How it
As in space
Determines some of our thought and actions

*

It is not possible to find logic of any sort
In Astrology
The idea that the canopy above
With the movement of the stars across the heavens
Coinciding with particular births
And even at times ordaining them
As well as predicting their future
Fails in any way that those who contend
Can call logical

In the early days
Whether people used the term
What they believed in was geo-centrism
And though some ancient civilizations
Understood better what was meant then
The Church on this earth in the middle centuries
Held people's thoughts in their grasp
Prolonging the long period
In which much of what surrounded us was denied
And those who thought otherwise were heretics and unbelievers

Then came a time when it was understood
The Sun was central to us
And as science developed there was the recognition
That the Sun
Our Sun
Was only one among many
And finally it was discovered
That there were different systems above us

It has been thought for some time
That we now know the origins of the Universe
We can discuss and argue
Yet I would still leave the question open
The one thing I would do however
Is rule out the thought of God
A thought coveted by humanity
To help people on their way
(As some believe)
It is by now not a useful answer
And it limits people

(I will not here discuss what some believe
To be a binding faith
Except to say something simple:
What binds us
If we can only admit it
Is our shared humanity)

*

Need we say
Life is Time past Time present and Time future?
Or are we all sensible enough to know this?
Even with obscure origins
We have science which has given us greater understanding of the Universe
There are those who look at history
Those only involved in the present
And those trying to grasp the future of us all
The planet and the stars
And what might happen through the forces involved

*

Perhaps I should finish with a few words
There was life
There were people
Some more primitive than today
We should at least refer to Darwin
As well as geologists and archaeologists
Whose thoughts span millennia
And the thoughts of God or gods were later
A development in the minds of humankind
In many ways a simple explanation for what has evolved

The cry of faith does not convince me
Though it is an element of many cultures
Today it can only hold us down

So if we say no God or gods
Do we only turn to Mammon?
A poor answer at any time

There is always the need for food and shelter for all
And some rest at times
But do not believe my disagreement with thoughts of God
Must mean only thoughts that are lean and mean

Think of what there is

I will leave it here

How measured should a conversation be?

To speak in a measured way can be admirable
Knowing what you're saying and why
It is something I would recommend to most people
Most of the time

Yet there are other times
And they may demand different approaches
Different ways of thinking
I in no way say
Use words of vitriol or hatred
The less of these the better
And if a feeling of anger comes over you
Be careful what you say
Try always not to be too loose in language

And speak in friendly fashion to your friends
Without condescension
While do not of a felt necessity hold back
On any analysis of a subject
You might be discussing

*

Understand
The measured tones of some may become boring
They may listen to themselves as they talk
And your part in the conversation may be neglected

Those who stand at podiums or pulpits
May impress themselves
With as is often said
The sound of their own voices

Avoid the pedant
The person who knows everything
It can be important to all of us
To know quite a lot
Certainly about the topic at issue
But overwhelming can become smothering
And the other no longer hears
Lost in a fog of emotion
So
Whatever the topic
It is times like this
That good sense kicks in
And your mind not always fully anchored
Drifts away from the subject

When this is so Time
Though not a commodity
But in many ways a precious asset
Can be wasted

However
If your thoughts go to pleasant pastures
It could be good to stay there for a while

(Perhaps until interest returns
And you hear the speaker's voice again)

How the West lost?

It could well be something to talk about
I would say not yet proven
Yet the numbers are going against what were once
The Great Western Powers

There is still some order there
Some organization and some achievement
Most leaders in the group consider themselves
To be of the top shelf
A cut (at least) above leaders
Of those that might still be called developing nations

There are of course ways we could delve into the question
Of the West losing itself
One would look at leaders such as Trump Boris Johnson
Scott Morrison and perhaps Orban
And if we include Russia in this grouping
Vladimir Putin

Watching a program by The Australia Institute
I was amused by Kishore Mahbubani
From the National University of Singapore
Who said the West was seriously in decline
Very past its best
And it was the many other countries outside the grouping
Who had come to prominence
He mentioned about 10 to 15%
Of the world's population existing in Western nations
And talked of the others making up the numbers

We can leave Kishore here for the moment
And say that even though many might not want to call

The others developed
It is true that their numbers grow
And with the form of globalization we have in the world
Most have some access to technology
And contact with the West as well

Some of the countries have developed technology themselves
And compete in the markets
And in the world
China and India are obvious examples
Japan is in a way more singular
And still has attachment (especially military)
With the United States

The fact that I recently read a book on Angela Merkel
Chancellor of Germany
Could be unfortunate
For while I was doing so I felt something
Perhaps an urge
To look again at Europe
Reconsider and bring myself up to date

This is not a spurious suggestion to myself
I have spent quite some time in the past studying European history
As well as spending a little living there

So yes I would like to know how Europe stands
Has the Union succeeded as some would have hoped?
Did Britain leaving do great harm
Or is continental Europe actually better off without them?
It could remain to be seen
While it is possible that Britain itself may flounder

As usual there are many aspects
Appertaining to a particular heading

[Though Europe is part of the Western powers
It no longer leads
I do not consider the EU inconsequential
But we are all aware today of the influence of NATO
A military body arching over it
And we are aware of the role the USA plays in this]

If we say as most would
The USA is of the West
We know that it is attempting to survive
Or at least save itself from the world around
And maintain what it considers to be its dominant position

I do not see it as the power it was
Or its citizens might believe it to be
It now more often turns to and relies on allies
Those the US believe are behind it
And support their views
There is something seriously unilinear
About the way they see the world
They may convince Australia a smaller power
But engaging with and attempting to use some of the Asian powers
Such as Japan and India
Might not work so well

In the minds of the Americans
And as their allies are supposed to believe
China and Russia are the demons
And even today the USA makes tentative approaches
To test China's mettle
It is possible that the allies seeing the USA's haphazard approach to them
And the world around may lose confidence in them

As some fair amount has been lost over time

If everybody in this world were sensible
They would avoid war
Yet not everybody including some leaders
Have the welfare of the whole world in their hearts
And sometimes not even the welfare of their own countries

*

I cannot approve of countries manufacturing
And selling armaments all over the world
I do not approve of the warlike comments
From opposing sides
I also say
That I could say
I do not understand why China is hardly recognized
As a Pacific power
Do not the members of the Quad believe China exists
Or is where it is
Or is the Quad really a flagrant attempt
To deal with China
To keep them out?

One can attempt to understand the USA
It has its history
It would be good for them to go back and look
Listen to themselves
And isolate the wrongs implicit in some of the many things they say
The claim of Manifest Destiny
The thought of their own Exceptionalism
The belief
In fact more explicit
That God is on their side
(And alongside that the foolish thought that they cannot lose)

Also we need to mention the allies

Firstly how many times has America determined UN actions?
Secondly
Are Japan Australia and India independent nations
Thinking for themselves?
Or are they following
Joining a group they believe will give them security
Without giving fair thought as to how and why?

[Thirdly I want to finish soon]

We could well ask
Who are up in arms?
The head of the US Congress visits Taiwan
Something I do not believe to be a wise move
It would in any objective sense be called provocative
Is the USA wishing for conflict?
I leave the question unanswered
Yet I am here in Australia
We
The country
Are said to be allied to the USA

All of us need to be more serious in asking what this means?

This morning I read that our newly minted Minister for Defence
Is calling for a review of Australia's defences
Exposing his thought of what might be the nation's inadequacies
In this regard

Some 3 days or so before the last Federal election
Which brought in (do I say)? My Party
The ALP
The now Deputy Prime Minister

Made a strong speech
About the dangers inherent in the China situation
I felt it to be over the top
And though he may have judged it politically necessary
I did not

At this point do I say
Have no defence
Let things happen as they will?
No
But we need to be wary of a world
That seems so edgy
Do I take a side?
Well I am in many ways ashamed
Of a Labor spokesperson advocating for more and more
Spending on defence

At the moment Labor is facilitating
The Voice to Parliament for Aboriginal people
I hope this means real progress

However for Labor to take up the cudgels
And become what many on the Right believe us to be
The last bastion of the West in the Pacific
Is a fact that can only be unfortunate for our country
And if we push the barrow
Unfortunate for the world

How we decipher situations

It is difficult at times not to take sides
Especially when you feel that what you might do
Or begin to do
Is indicate support for someone or something
That alienates you from your own people

This I do not want to do

But as I often say
I'm getting tired
And now more so

I could ask some simple questions
Not necessarily the right ones
But they might indicate that not all is well
In the State of Denmark
Or in any state for that matter

I heard a commentator say yesterday
That Russia was carrying on the Cold War
Yet is this an accurate portrayal?
Could it be that the West is pushing hard
And Vladimir has got into some form of paranoid state?

Essentially he is an intelligent man
As intelligent as the Western leaders
Yet the USA and Europe
Especially the USA
Somehow wish to grind Russia into the dust
And in this the Baltic states and Ukraine
Have been part of their deployment

I am not usually an attacking person
So I refrain from full explanation
Yet I fail to see that it is not evident
How the USA has pushed its influence East
Further through Europe
And further pushed its ideology onto Ukraine
At times its officials helping them in their elections
And continually putting forth the bait of NATO membership

It is certainly right that Russia believes it has rights to part of Ukraine
But we need to recognize that the USA in its own way exerts influence

We are supposed to accept the terms geostrategic or geopolitical
Yet if we do it more than likely forces us
And among us many small to middle order nations
To give up any idea of self-determination

So Ukraine and its President
Might believe it will decide its own fate
Yet to a large degree it will be the major powers
Pushing and pulling on either side
That will do so

America hangs out its idea of a currency of freedom
Yet America is hardly free
So will those in Ukraine have control of their own country
After the dust has settled
Or will the tentacles of NATO
That is in fact not just a defensive grouping
But an explicitly military one?
Today as its members commit themselves
To higher Defence budgets
The worry in the world must only grow greater

(There are many military groupings
Of which we should ask
In whose name do they exist and act?
And to what purpose?)

I think it best to leave this matter for the moment
But I feel it necessary to ask once again:
Is it only Putin who has chosen to fight this terrible war
Over the country near to its borders
Or are there greater forces at play behind all this?

I will say something simple

A week or so ago I had a conversation with a man
Someone I do not know well
I do know him
But had forgotten his name
The question of global warming came up
And he was I would be prepared to say
A climate change denialist
Though I little like to typify people thus
He could only consider the thought of perhaps there being
A very hot year in say 1938
So he considered there was no need to deal with people's predictions
Apparently he knew better
I do not know how schooled he was or is
As is usual I did not want to pursue a futile discussion
There was no thought of polar ice melting
Or rainforests being decimated
Or rising seas swamping islands
No he thought the answer was simple
We are clever
We solve problems all the time

I did not really wish to engage in a discussion
About humanity's success
And dominance over nature
And even perhaps beyond that
I did not want to hear the refrain
Often uttered
Usually little thought out

Yet I do not damn the gentleman for his views

I sit here now and write a little
And there's a reason for that

Who are these clever people who will save us?
If he pays no heed to the warnings
Of most of the world's climate scientists
The clever ones must be others
So are they our leaders?
We can ask this of course
And at the same time know
The leaders though they say they move with the times
Always try to maintain the status quo
Economics essentially involves growth
Or so they say
And such a thought does not help

What we need is some form of sustainable reality around the world

*

Here in Australia
I believe
As many others do
The present Coalition government's energy policy
Is more gloss than anything
To the Prime Minister presentation is what matters
And though he repeats again and again
The thought of achieving zero emissions by 2050
We know he is a person who believes in miracles
And it can only be that his policy can succeed
If somehow there is some divine intervention
For Scomo and his cohort have put little thought
Into making the world safe for us

A Prime Minister who hugs and holds people
Gregarious and jovial and confident in himself
Is not enough

I believe we should listen to no more talk of miracles from him
Put God aside
And look towards a government of integrity and worth
One which works steadily for the whole country
Considering those of all ages and groupings
And is able to understand what it's doing

In Australia's interest?

(1)

Let us drop the thought of the Indo-Pacific area
And look at the Pacific Ocean
For the moment
It's large and touches many countries
As well as involving a large number of islands

I say involve because there are other matters
Than just the great ocean
There are countries which are vying for position there
We do not need to name them all
Many people are aware of what's going on
Though it's certainly interesting the Australian Coalition government
Hardly seemed to take many of our nation's interests seriously
As well as neglecting those of our neighbours'

There are so many sides to the situation
I can only mention a few

For a start I will take one
And mention the newly appointed Shadow Minister for Defence
Though I state I do not like wars
I grant that such things exist
Though hopefully as few as possible
The gentleman in question served in the SAS in Afghanistan
Between 2010 and 2015

I do not expect it would have been an easy time
And acknowledge it would be part of what gives him
Intelligence and some knowledge of war there and elsewhere

As well as the conditions under fire
I'm sure some comradeship would be involved
In a place where your life (or death) might rely on it

Mr Hastie has written an opinion piece relating to some of
his experiences
Brief of course
Not every aspect can be covered

His piece is essentially divided
Though he may not see it this way
Firstly he talks of the wrong that some of those
Who have often been considered elite soldiers
Have committed overseas
He mentions countries other than Australia
Yet in the early part of the article
He focuses on what some Australians might have done
And expresses support for the Brereton Report
On some more than unfortunate happenings in Afghanistan
He praises the report
But unfortunately he makes it appear that it has been acted on
By the authorities
And further into his article he mentions
The defamation case brought against some Australian publishers

It should be pointed out that there are members of the public
Who believe the defamation case was an attempt on the part
Of one of the soldiers mentioned in the report
To stall what many would have believed to be
The necessary condition:
A due and honest investigation into the Report itself

I will say again
I do not like wars
Though I am aware of how much many countries

Are invested in them
But there are things that could be done
For one: completely disband the SAS

I have read closely the papers on the defamation trial
And they present a picture of a branch of the army
That is hardly doing service for the country
Elite they may be said to be
But I find in the reading there is considerable evidence
Of brutality in approach
Not only towards the enemy
But towards their fellow soldiers as well

In the case as it is presented in the paper
I am as certain as I can be
That I would find against the soldier who instigated it
However I am neither lawyer nor judge
Yet there are times the public needs to judge a situation
For its own understanding
And as a person who pays attention to what goes on
At times I feel a strong need to write about it

So best to leave the issue at the moment
While stating emphatically the necessity
Of the Brereton Report being made accessible to the public
As well as being subject to a full judicial investigation

(2)

Now Karl Marx is by no means the only person
Who pointed out and attempted to resolve
Some of the world's contradictions
There have been others tackling such problems

Andrew Hastie however is hardly able
To take full on the contradiction he presents
To us of the wrongs done by elite soldiers
And the necessity as he sees it of identifying enemies

From his position the thought of enemies
Could well be obvious
Yet it is passing strange his answers for dealing with them:
2 terms stand out in the way he believes
We must contest with and defeat these enemies
The phrases are hard power
And lethal force

It is amazing that the Shadow Minister for Defence
Is not aware of what he's saying
These sayings
Mantras that they are in the Armed Forces
Are what the SAS has been involved in
They are a part of the force he condemns for its wrong-doing
In the many countries of the world

Is he so foolish as to think
That he with his words of integrity
And complaint about the wrongs of the Special Forces
Would wipe the slate clean?

There I dust my hands
That's done

Now we can start again
And people will by then understand
That military hard power and lethal force are acceptable

Involvement

Val once asked me why I have never written about her
It is of course not so
She has been involved in some things I've done
Mainly years ago

I have also over the last 2 years or so
Done 3 or 4 short pieces about Val and me
I would consider them little revealing
Though they do have at least some relation to the truth
Without going into any detail

For now I will mention later years
Though I must note we first met at the Student Union at Monash
In 1965
And talked for quite some time
Believing perhaps both of us thought
We hit it off

But leave beginnings
And intermediate years

We split up around 1972
Though it may have been before
No-one would be sure
She was not happy
And I cannot say how committed either of us was

Though I was in an unfortunate state in 72
I believe it was then
That Val and David married
I'm sure they had their ups and downs

But it did seem to me
As we had remained friends
That they were well suited

David and Val I believe (in my own mind)
Supported me in my lonely years
And after I met Alannah
The four of us would get together at times

This continued over the years
By this time David and Val had been reasonably successful
In business
David having designed a surgical dressing
This interested people in China
Who took it up
Thereafter David designed the factories as well
And Val
Having learnt Mandarin to some extent
As well as studying Chinese history
Would produce the instruction manuals needed

It might all sound good and well
They were successful
And fairly well off

Eventually they bought a 2 acre block in Donvale
Had a large house built and lived there
When Alannah and I visited
Usually Lans would go off and talk with Dave
And Val who was a keen and knowledgeable gardener
Would take me to see and appreciate the garden
Surrounding the house

We had some good dinners

Val and Dave had a daughter Siri
Whom I had known from birth

Yet there was the sad side to all of this
David had Hodgkin's disease
And though I'm not sure when he was told
He was beyond it
He then developed some secondary growths
By this time his immune system was shot
And he was never really well again

He died about 8 years ago

Val delivered the eulogy
It is time ago now
But I remember how well she did it

There are other truths involved

With David hardly able to work for years
Their earnings diminished
About 4 to 5 years ago Val bought a house in Blackburn
Where their first house had been
It needed work
And she could not afford to create a garden overnight
It would take her time
And with her bad back and increasing age
It was slow going

Also as I've told people
Though I do not vouch for the truth of it
I have mentioned
She would like me back
This could be true
But I am not the young man of 55 years ago

Unfortunately Val has been slow making friends
Though she has Siri and her 3 children
And they're close emotionally

What is it that matters in this life?
Time waves its wand over all
Some experience of the past remains with us
But usually it is the more recent
That remains at hand

It is not always easy for a person to live on his or her own
Yet at times they must
I have tried over time to encourage Val to go out
And talk to people when there's an opportunity
Her tendency is to say I can do it
But she can't

But there is still time
And it's best not to leave the possibility of contact too late
Everywhere there are cafes libraries and meeting places

At Monash Uni she started
Though did not finish
A MA thesis on a Welsh writer Richard Hughes
Perhaps she should take up the words of Dylan Thomas
(Reprobate though he was):
Do not go gentle into that good night
Old age should burn and rave at close of day
Rage, rage against the dying of the light

Keep it brief

Labor has been in government federally
For over 2 months
They are doing what they can
A large number of matters are being dealt with
And most of the promises they made before the election
Will be dealt with
It has the feel of a Labor government
Something I welcome
But we cannot always be happy

I will not enumerate the good points
Just mention the great disappointment
The commitment and furthering of looking at Defence
Being prepared to raise the budget for it
And all in all adopting a more militant stance
Than I would like

I have a great regard for Paul Keating the former Prime Minister
Keating says we should involve ourselves in our region
But Richard Marles now the Minister for Defence
Firm and stern of face
About 3 days before the election spoke of China
And its threat
So said he
We must be prepared

At the moment that is all I will say
Except to mention the review that those involved in Defence
Are putting together
In regard to our needs and the possible strengthening
Of our forces

The Defence Minister's statement is that the Pacific
Is a complex strategic situation
And we must face it

I could call this bluster
Yet the man is Deputy Prime Minister
It would be expected we should take him seriously

We know China wants access to the Pacific
And that it wants to spread its influence in the area
But Australia has already chosen
And we will if we continue in this way
Never have autonomy

Perhaps I'm a little basic here
I do not regard the Americans as mates
And for many years have been aware
Of times they have illustrated to the world their aggression
And what they believe to be their dominance

*

However I conclude with a few simple thoughts
That attempt some form of objectivity
In which we remember we are here in our Island state
Australia

There is a strong tendency today
For governments to use such terms as geostrategic
Or geopolitical
And situate their thoughts in the middle of what these words indicate
I prefer that we handle others with tact and diplomacy
Not giving in to them
But being creative in our mutual obligations

Though I am getting on in age
And may not live to see it
I know what would be left of the Australian people
(If there were any at all)
If we took up arms
Especially in the cause of others
Those left
Probably few
Would never forgive an Australian government
That took them into war

Law and Morality

Perhaps I should write a long piece
About my problem in approaching Law
How I consider what is essentially important
Is not the legal judgement
But the moral understanding of life and our part in it

This all needs to be ably worked out
Not just sketched in

In your early years you get a sense
Of what moral order is
And you work at it
Trying to understand how and why it is so

It is not a moral universe
Unfortunately we cannot say that
The morality involved is with all of us
Acting and inter-acting with other humans
As well as animals
And the world itself

There is no doubt that there are
And will be
Many acts involving the physical world which do harm
We must question the morality of these

*

Consider sophistical and adversarial arguments
Are they properly designed to find the truth of a situation?
Many points may be brought out by the barristers
In their engagement

While there may be some of importance neglected
Because they do not fit the shaping that is done
(And there will be times when the barristers really do have no answer)

So the single view:
A judge without a jury?
No jury to weigh up the evidence
To weigh up and if necessary debate
Is another matter that leads me to an uncertainty about the law
How much confidence can the society have in judges?
We hear of
We know of
Poor judgements

It may appear prosaic but the questions need to be asked
Do these judges have greater knowledge than the general public
Greater intellectual skills and discernment?
At times we are not convinced

However we must say
Or at least assume
That their focus on the facts
Or the questions involved
Should give them a decided advantage

Linear logic

The truth is I sometimes find my critical faculty
Taking over at times it might be better not to
In a group today I was saying something
And a member accused me of not following logical process
This type of talk appals me
When people say it they are often extremely limited in their view
They adhere to a linear logic
And do not realize how this rules out
A full appreciation of the world
And for that matter even the conversation of others

If logic were purely linear
That is if it were not related to reason
I feel many people would keep walking in their straight line
Towards the cliff
And like lemmings many would follow
And they would probably all just unwittingly fall over

To tell a story you need to collect the parts
And put them together in some way
It's obvious you will need some sequence
But this need not always dictate the line of the story
For a story needs much more than that
It is a way of filling the world

With the language we've all developed
It needs be collective
But some care for it more than others
Braggarts speak loudly
Yet we often do not listen
At times quiet words are more meaningful

We see colour in the world
In nature as well as people and their doings
And the colour does not exist in a logical sense
It is something our senses respond to
So red and green are there to be seen
And many more we do not name
Until they become necessary in what they convey

Look both ways

It is certainly best not to think
How good you are
Nor should you enhance any thought of this kind
When people comment on you or your ability

You are only as good as you can be
And that is up to you

There are numerous ways of relating to others
And as many ways of not relating

If you're gregarious it's likely you will talk
To many people often
Though always we know this will not
Or cannot go on forever
There is a time to stop

And there is of course
Something we all know
A time to turn away
This may sound cruel
But that is not the intention
Yet we know we cannot talk
Cannot deal with everybody
And certainly not all the time

*

Yes we all turn away at times
Not wishing to see the other
Or to talk
At other times there might be something to be said

But the words freeze in your mind
Or you know it's best not said

Do many people have an over-riding judgement
When meeting people
As to what to say
And what not?

When this judgement is determined by a form
Of class difference
I am unhappy about it
An uneasy unhappiness which will because of your make-up
Force some words out

This can be so
Who is to know?
The outcome need not be acrimonious
We go through these trials often
Over the days weeks and years
And yes if we have any sense
We do learn!

Meaning alongside purpose

In a conversation with a friend
I believe it was Leonard
Because we have had some talks of the nature
I will mention
He said with an assumption in what he said
That I had a purpose in life
Something to that effect
Recording is not always perfect
Often quite a lot less so
But what we were talking about was in this area
As I can be prone to do
I hesitated slightly
I need not say I equivocate about the question or my answer
Yet I know to have some purpose
Proper purpose
Purpose of a worthwhile kind
We need to have some meaning in our lives

For the moment I will leave the naming
Of this meaning open
And say I believe there are many things
That can provide it
Even dare I say faith in some thing or person

Often faith gets a bad innings in my view of life
But it is necessary to understand
I do not ridicule it
Though in many ways I do not agree with the faith of many
Essentially I baulk at religious faith
When it stands as a barrier
Or bulwark
Against any thinking that may oppose it

However I have written of such matters at other times
So best to say
Let those who have faith have it
As long as it is not bigotry

I have also in the past
Sketched out at some length
Many things that can be meaningful to us
So I will not do so again here

Yet I refer to some important points in our lives
Either people thoughts or happenings
Which sustain us through what may be bad times
Because we know of the worth they have

I am not the greatest worker
But know this
We all need to work at life
Not in a stressful fashion
But being as relaxed as possible
While keeping in mind our important touchstones

There are ways to find them
Essentially we need to attempt to understand
What makes humanity worthwhile
And attempt to be part of it

Isolation and alienation happen to many people
But the need to overcome the difficulties
Is common to us all
States of being
Be they ever so many
Are not exclusive to a select few

At this point I will say adieu

Menzies years ago spoke of the Forgotten People

I would not agree with the premise he had
Yet I among others believe the thought of the Silent Majority

And why does it not speak
Not formulate
Not present views to the rest of us?
People need political activity
They should have some engagement
And speak up for themselves
Encouragement helps

Could they
Would they
Be the famous tipping point?
The people finding their voices
To say enough is enough

We see leaders hardly capable of leading
Not necessarily timid
But leading us away from our survival

Burn coal and gas
Produce more and more
What will be the outcome?
We see how in many ways politicians and lobbyists are let loose
Despite what many think there are groups continuing
To pursue their own ends

*

The present Federal Energy Plan is very much a small letter plan
Do as little as they can
For as long as they can get away with it

More unfortunate days!

(1)

Sean died last Tuesday
The next Saturday I had great pain all night
With a bowel blockage
The next day Alannah said she would take herself to Joan's
Instead of my taking her
She'd catch the train

At 6.30pm she rang and asked if I would pick her up at Joan's
On the way to the station she had fallen on some uneven pavement
And broken 2 and a half of her upper front teeth

And now last Saturday
After a day of ill-health
She fainted on her way to the back toilet
Falling straight backwards
When she attempted to roll over I saw the blood
A large amount and a smaller closer to where she had turned
And seeing her on her side
I could make out blood plastered over the back of her head
Her hair matted
I got her up
Awkward as I am
By this time she was fairly conscious
But could hardly help
Actually making it more difficult than it would be
For a man of my age
76 and a bad back and overall too many operations

Simon and I took her to the hospital
And she was admitted the next day

She came out yesterday
Thursday
I have tried to tell her
By re-enforcing what the doctor had told her
To get as much rest as possible
She agrees
But feels she's needed to contribute to the details
Of Sean's funeral

I have cancelled my operation for next Friday
I'm not confident
As well I have DVT
And am on blood thinners

So all in all it has not been a good time of late
Yet everybody is coping

(2)

Underneath all this
Last evening St Kilda were beaten by what was said to be
A lowly Essendon
Friday night and it made for a very unfortunate week

Whether it's an empty feeling or a desperate one
I am beginning to feel I cannot go on watching the team fail
For all the days of my life
I feel forever let down
What is it we supporters are hoping for?
It may be alright for the successful clubs over all these years
But 1 premiership in all this time
And not another in sight

Distraught no
Desperate no
But I feel I can hardly go on supporting a team
That disappoints me so often

I'll never go to another match
The last I was at was in 2010
When we lost the Grand Final to Collingwood
Today my back is so bad
As is my walking
And I know I could not handle the crowds

So perhaps I should cut my ties
And say it was a failed enterprise
For almost the 73 years of my life I've followed them

Need we always be refined?

Bullshit!
That's a start

Watching a program 2 hours long on Australia
In a series called
A thousand years of history
At first it seemed reasonable enough in its presentation
There was much we already knew of the land
Though it can be that many of our thoughts are second-hand

Yet it finally takes up the question of the nation
And the binding necessary for us
And where it began
According to the historians presenting the program
Those I often call the Talking Heads
What formed us as a nation was war
The Boer War is not mentioned
Though there seemed to be some film from that time
But Gallipoli
Thought to be the testing ground
The crucible
Forged in war we came through

So are we to believe it is this that makes Australia?
Or is it the idea of warriors
Male warriors
Fighting and killing
And we in this future of ours
Are to see them as heroes?

None of the historians question the thought
Of war's necessity in the birth of a nation

What do programs such as this do?
Get together a group of historians
Who accept the wars
The reality or the necessity?

And once these historians present this view
They can go on
And list further conflicts
In which (they believe) Australians have been prominent and strong
And over time pivotal to our concept of Australianness

Now is not the time to list them
But at least to say there are those who study history
Who do not take war for granted
And do not of necessity laud the abilities of our own soldiers

Yes we had Japanese submarines in Sydney Harbour
And Darwin was bombed
I was not alive then
(Almost but not quite)!
But am aware of how the Australian people must have felt
With the dangers at hand

I do not ridicule the soldiers
But emphasize what has largely been a male initiative
Into war
Though now women are encouraged to join the Defence forces
It's a job
Perhaps a career
Many are encouraged by the government figures involved:
The leaders

I did not go to Vietnam
For the horrible encounters there
I was not chosen
But best not to be

Around that time I was driving cabs at night
And had a role
Not of course propaganda
But one where I stayed informed about SE Asia
And what was happening
And talked to passengers about the situation
No I was not fighting just talking
But my research was a little more thorough
Than that of the newspapers of the time

So perhaps I contributed something

And I knew war was wrong
And I knew that the Vietnam War was particularly wrong

My young brother was one of the chosen
So?
He went underground for most of the time

Towards the end of the War
Just before the Whitlam Labor Government was voted in
He was in gaol for a week
For handing out anti-war pamphlets in the city

I know some men who suffered badly from it all
And there are some who took their own lives

This idea of War which many believe to be good
Is anything but
The response to the authorities controlling these matters
Should be to say no
Be sensible
Be diplomatic towards other countries
And only when you absolutely must act
Do so

There are today in this country
Those with loud voices
They speak out
And some are convinced
But in the quiet of night
We can realize
Many of these people are only talking up war

[Another way of saying it is:
Be careful
There are war-mongers in our society]

Not cranky but…

(1)

I wanted to watch the Test cricket against Sri Lanka
This afternoon
But inadvertently found myself looking at
A tribute to Shane Warne
It reminded me strongly of what a great bowler he was
Exceptional and with his own inimitable way of doing things
Watching him bowl
I realized I could not admire a spin bowler more
Than I did he

I had my car serviced yesterday
And the driver from Brighton Mazda dropped me off
At Mandoline's for lunch
Alannah and I had discussed whether I would be able to walk
The one kilometre home
She considered it too much for me
But I thought I'd try it
Without the car only walking would get me home
So I walked
Fairly strongly in the early stages
Feeling confident that with the help of my cane
I could do it
Yet as I walked and began to feel the stress of it
I realized one thing I had hoped for on the way
Was not available
I had thought there would be some reasonably low brick walls
So I could have a short rest
But no
All the fences were high pickets
Or upright metal bars
I can only suppose to protect the inmates from such as me

Or all the hoi polloi around
It's a shame the prevalence of such thoughts
If such they are
Not only keeping me out
But people going past
I can only suppose the people feel secure
Behind the palisades
(Or are they barricades)?

Has the concept of neighbourliness almost entirely gone
At least in our suburb?
If so how sad this is
And how sad the people who have created this environment

*

Let us leave secluded people behind sad fences
And talk of St Kilda
They won last night in the major Friday night game
Beating Carlton by 15 points
Most would have expected Carlton to be the victors
Yet they kicked badly for goal and generally were not as convincing
As we were
St Kilda had lost 3 games in a row
While Carlton I had described to a couple of people during the week
As rampant
But we took the initiative from the start
And despite the injuries suffered during the match
They were full of spirit
Moving the ball with intensity
And obviously wanting the win

Afterwards in the clubrooms we saw their enthusiasm
And the belief they'd learnt something from the lesson
Of the last 3 weeks

(2)

This morning I started to mourn
The fact that I am thwarted from writing at the moment
And cannot pursue my usual habits
Yes I have written something tonight
Though I would probably not put great store in it
But at least it gets my blood flowing
Or should I say my pen moving?

I'd watched TV till about 12
Falling asleep for the last half hour or so
And I thought
What would I be doing at that time
If not thwarted in the house?
It would be obvious
I would collect some thoughts of the day together
And put them down in the form that suited me
But as I knew this
I also knew that I could not do it in full fashion
My house is not mine
I have for the moment lost the ability to think
As I move from room to room
From activity to activity
And I suddenly realized the way
The essential way
In which this is not good

(3)

Since I met them 2 people have helped me out
Of the stagnation I was in
First Alannah
And then Barney

Whatever I say of Alannah I do not forget this debt to her
Nor do I forget Barney's influence

They both helped me in many ways
I cannot number them
But as far as writing goes
Around the time Alannah and I met in the early 80's
She with a few words encouraged me to finally work at
And get a degree
The whole experience re-asserted a confidence in me
I had not had fully for years

So there was some worthwhile and finished background
In Academia
Also Barney moved my thought on
As well as in some ways forcing me to matters of my past
That I had neglected

After we met
Not long after Alannah and I came to Elsternwick
We talked regularly over coffee and often walked together
Though Barney's knowledge and understanding of politics
In Australia was so much greater than mine
We shared the interest
And after we'd got to know each other better
He would repeat the refrain:
You should write

It took a form of hyper-manic state
To open my mind further
But his words had had the effect
And the 2 weeks I spent in the clinic
Were not so bad
I only waited to get out
And resume my life outside
While knowing some drive in me had re-surfaced
And become over time an established meaning for me

Of essential importance

The planet and the plants and the creatures thereon
And understanding of time
And change over time
As well as space
Is there sufficient here for us all
On the planet?
Or are we becoming crowded?

Some absolutes might be considered essential
For instance, love

Yet the consideration we know we need must extend to all

Stop the wars /Let nations settle

Love (or whatever it may be) can take time
And related feelings may develop
So many of today's thoughts are not helpful to anyone
Either the young or the old
But yes we do need to learn
And if we care there is so much
Of essential importance
To humanity

One among many

Questions abound in this world
Or they should
Abound and rebound
And many need to be answered
But how often are they not
Not answered by anyone
Not even considered

Over time the neglected questions of years before
Are resurrected by people
And asked again

Is there any way to solve this problem of randomness?
Or do we just accept it
Only on occasions coming to face matters
At other times ignoring them

We do have major questions in the above context
Where do the important ones come from?
Is the current media adequate to the task
Or is much of it just glitter and entertainment
Keeping us engaged as we go through life
With little thought to what needs to be thought?

I am a writer
A writer of sorts
Hardly great
Nor would I want to be
Though I have read many of those considered to be above the ruck

There are many other writers
In many different fields
There are those who deal with the world around
Some write fiction
Some poetry
And there are those who observe and comment
On a wide range of matters

There is a wide range of ability among us all

Yet I feel fairly confident in saying that many of these writers
Are insular
Thinking their own thoughts
Or seeking their own ways to understand the world

*

To cut this short:
I must ask
How many consider the thoughts of others
Other writers of course
But also the people they meet in the shops or cafes and restaurants
Or on the streets?

*

The question is: Who listens?

Outside or in: where do thoughts come from?

I am sitting here once again
And have had an argument
Even though the gentleman has been polite
He has said I'm biased
And have a wrong view of history
Of course I would say whatever he is saying
Is that mine is different to his

One could ask where our thoughts come from?
How well are we trained or educated?
Do we think mainly in line with what prevails in our culture
Either that dominant or others existing alongside
In the society?

*

We were talking about global warming
He did not seem terribly concerned
According to him we are clever
People are clever
Obviously if there are problems we solve them
Or will
Though my view is that at times it's necessary to ask when?

There are many instances of answers coming after the time required
This can be too late
What good is cleverness then?

Drop a line as I have just done
And ask the further question
Does this cleverness extend to all humankind?

How do we resolve situations we have let go on
For too long?

Perhaps we should go back to the predication of cleverness
Is it something we see in our leaders
Those who do not respond to the needs of the people
Or the planet
The leaders may have started off with some ideals
But in the political hurly-burly
Have thoughts only of themselves and their cohorts
Those keeping them in power

What is left behind?
Who is left behind?
Who suffers?
Who dies?

Will it be the result of some people's lies?

Pardon me

I don't know what to say
Or how to say it
I do not argue that I'm living among aliens
Yet my house is no longer my home
Don't think I have no sympathy for the others here
And the trials they have undergone
Losing their brother
As well as illness in the family

Yet despite sympathy
And some understanding
I am unhappy
This is not what I'm used to
Our family home when I was young was different
The Kelly family the siblings are close
But the truth is they relate differently to each other
Than I do to my brothers

I would say we
The 3 brothers though family
Are perhaps more distant
Or not forever intimate in our relations as are the Kellys
We talk about organizational matters at times
But not always
And I know through experience
We would not want to live together at this age
For any sustained period of time

Where is communication to be had in this world
In this house
Or any house?
What are matters of interest?
My brothers and I are concerned with each other's health

And we share an interest in history
Giving such books to each other on birthdays and at Christmas
We also have financial ties
Though they don't do much for me
I need to keep involved

Yet with the Kellys it seems it's their youthful experience
And affection
That keeps them together
Sometimes I have the sense they've never got away from them

Yes I know
I'm unfair in my criticism
My heart can be wrenched at times
And I find it difficult to talk about matters
Some of which almost bring tears to my eyes
Probably there is little right or wrong in this
But at the same time I can feel trapped
And see no way out
And that is not good

I could express fear of my getting upset
But know I will probably hold on for the time necessary
I know also that I should see David Weissman again soon
If he will see me
But there is no perfect antidote

I am old
I cannot run away
Or make a new home elsewhere
And home matters to me

Are we swamped now in this house?
Have we been invaded?
Must I keep my mouth shut about the truth?
The truth I know
The truth for me

People should know

The monarchy is an insult to our country
And those recognizing it take part
It's easy to say she's a lovely woman
Old and intelligent
Loved by all
But truth often lives elsewhere than in the many words uttered

The wish to acknowledge the Platinum Jubilee
As being of significance
Has been taken up by some of Australia's media
Yet we know of this Queen
And her correspondence
That almost certainly showed some culpability
In the letters exchanged between her and Sir John Kerr
About the dismissal of the Whitlam Labor Government

These letters were kept from the Australian people
Until last year
When Professor Jenny Hocking
After years of attempting to do so
Forced the correspondence to be released
Through Australia's National Archives

The Archives showed little willingness to allow this
But Professor Hocking persisted

We
The Australian people
Would like to think such matters were not kept from us
While some in our society would like us to believe
In the innocence of the British Monarch

I see it differently
The monarch was never innocent
And throughout history Kings and Queens have not been
But have worked to sustain their own positions

There are those of us who say of us
And accept
That we are settlers in this land
Perhaps the word applies
We all know or should
Of the wrongs done to the Original Peoples here
And the wrongs were compounded
In the bodies of the settlers too
Many sent here chained or indentured
Yes we were a convict colony

And those who sent our forebears
Were directed by the Upper Classes
Of the late 19th century and beyond
The Kings and Queens and aristocracy having a say
In the prevailing judgements
Against poorer people
Much poorer
The lower classes

So why do we (or some of us)
Revere the monarchy?

There is no simple answer
But it is helpful to know something
About the evolution of Rule in a Kingdom
And the taxes gathered
And the estates and wealth owned
By the upper classes

History will tell us nothing
Unless we study it

*

The Queen is not the Queen of my country
She is 96 and I congratulate her for that
But if I were to send her a message
I would wish her all the best for her 96th year
While saying that sensibly I do not recognize her here
Either her rule
Or any constitutional right

Let her keep to her own country
If her people will have her
And let her give up any thoughts of interfering with Australia
Either because she believes she has station here
Or her wealth along with her power
Would help her

In whatever way I might represent Australia
I (whose mother was English)
Wish her no harm

But desire no continuation of the thoughts
Of the British Royal charm and significance

Finally:
She has lived through 95 years
So without ridicule
I can only suggest that now might be the time (if she is ever able)
To realize and understand how many here in Australia feel:
There should be no Kings and Queens

Polyglot?

(1)

It could be said that each nation is singular
Yes it could be said
Yet would it be worth saying?

I'm sure we could isolate some features of countries
Wherein there might be something special
But what is more likely to be is its history as well as its economy
And natural resources
With the development of the society over time
And the changing borders that define the nation

Yet do they?

Let us move away from the physical term
The singularity of nation or humanity
And point out and then keep in mind
The polyglot nature of any society we know of

Once upon a time
Not really all that long ago
There was a bookshop in Elizabeth Street Melbourne
I remember it
Though not well
But recall the name: Polyglot Books

I'm fairly sure I went in a number of times
Certainly the name intrigued me
Memory
That is my memory
Tells me it had books on a wide range of languages

Being much younger then than I am now
That was a further enticement
Though I speak only English
Or it and the Australian version of it
I do have an interest in language generally
The genesis of
The formation of
Also the diversity
There is similarity among many of them
Harking back millennia

Wherever people come from
We mention the Indo-European language
As being thought to be pervasive
Yet our thought should range wider than that

The origins of writing
Or looking back further
The origins of language
We keep searching for

As far as the development of writing goes we have a good idea
Much work has been done
But language?
The origins are not clear cut
And when we think about it
We need to consider many features
Though some people may see them as external
Yet we need to know the origins of humanity matter in this search
And physical social and cultural anthropology

No in this situation we do not have easy answers
While at the same time it is certainly worthwhile
To mention that some words
That have been included in the lexicon for millennia
May well have dubious roots

Perhaps planted there by those who in their own way
Accumulated power
And hence control over others

Either the words
Or the names of the people who promulgated them
Might be more suspect
Than many in the world today would acknowledge

(2)

This is not a certain fact
But let us assume that many Americans
As people in other countries
Claim unity
And are proud of it
Yet we know underneath this unity
The swearing in of the President
And the on-going claims of their all being democratic
There is disunity and discord
There is disenchantment
And poverty
And racial divide
Nothing is absolute
Yet words are often used as if they are
God bless America
One would assume it would include all of them

*

Keep us in conversation here
Somewhere in the modern day…

Barak Obama talked of the Covenant
An agreement
And of course you would expect some agreement came about

But Obama was there and then he was not
And Trump came
Whatever he might or might not have done on the world stage
He cared nothing for any Covenant
The divide became greater

So we see beneath the claims the country makes
There is division between different groupings
The North and the South still not reconciled
And East and West distant
As must be many of the voices of their people
And their Congress people
As they are heard across the nation

Yet God is still somehow called to bless the nation
Involved in the blessing are many curses often unrecognized
Take evil
Something considered by many religious people
As existing
Existing outside or beyond people

Yet there need only be the recognition
That it is humanity that creates evil
And it should not
Definitely should not
Something we find easy to say
But only to say
Though we know it to be the answer

(3)

Is it the concept of unity that is wrong
One nation undivided?
Do we need to move away from the singular thought
To recognize

What we should already know
Most nations are polyglot in language and customs
People have been dispersed across the world for millennia
And it is still so

What was neglected in the Old World
With the creation of Empires
And then their fall
And in the so-called New World
Are the different voices in the world

We have a need to know
Among both those with voice
And those able to support them

Rip Van Winkle

I have said it before
Yet now I count it
Between 1972 and 2006
I wrote only about 10 poems
Short and sweet?
Maybe

I have also said I was asleep for that time
Not entirely true
I was rehabilitating myself
Learning to live in an acceptable way
For both me and others
Of course others helped
And I needed them
And needed to look around
And see and hear and talk
In fact re-discover and re-use my senses
Without going off the deep end again

This last resolve did not hold me fully
Yet the occasions were less severe
And I did come back to some stability

What was this stability?
A form of personal and social consciousness that allowed me to be
Without fully compromising myself

I could number people who helped me
Some willingly some inadvertently
And on occasions I have named them
But the truth is as I gained confidence

I met many people
And though they may well not know this
They played their part in my drama

*

You may think it odd or wrong
Calling my life a drama
Yet I have lived it and know
That it is in many ways
Both drama and comedy
As well at times farce
An absurdist approach could well sum it up
In the way it does us all
Touching on all facets
When I was younger much was seen as absurd
Yet since then with the changing times
We should have the sense to uncover
Layer after layer

I say layer after layer
And what is involved is the mass the crowd
As well as community and the personal

As a child I thought as a child
Apparently
I'm not really sure what that means
I do know I was active physically in the 2nd grade
My teacher spoke to my mother
About my undue activity
So I was supposed to realize that that was what I was engaged in
At the same time when meeting people
Mum would often say I was shy
And perhaps I was
I met people but did not immediately have something to say

There was perhaps the eternal excuse that I started school at 4
It did me no particular harm
But it meant I was always younger than others in my class

I'm not sure if I understood it at the time
Yet I know I mightily regretted leaving St Kilda
The area I was born and bred in
The football team I barracked for
And the school and friends I had a great love for

My last term of primary school was at Bentleigh West
I didn't like it
St Kilda was supposed to be a rough place
But some of those in Bentleigh were crude
A couple of them wanted to fight me
I was small and the new kid on the block
But I had decided I'd had enough of fighting
At St Kilda by the time I left I was the best fighter in the school
So eventually nobody picked on me
This was a far healthier situation than the niggardly kids
At Bentleigh at the time

So in leaving Bentleigh I was glad to go to Brighton High
And once again come into my own
I seemed to talk to a good many people
And was interested in them all
I understood then we were all the same
Though different
No matter where we came from
Make an effort communicate
Something will happen

All went swimmingly in my first 5 years at Brighton
And then disaster struck

For years I enjoyed the lessons
The teachers and the learning
And was in my own way getting somewhere
Maths English the Sciences and Humanities
Were all of interest
And I did well
And that may have been my downfall

I was also a prefect and House Captain
In a House that was by no means brilliant at sport
But won in Drama year after year

So I leave these cursory notes
Remember my view that after Brighton
I like Rip Van Winkle slept (or slumbered)

Or if one wants other words
I was in the wilderness for years
Without really being aware

There were those around who helped me

To understand the disaster that struck me
You will find I allude to it here and there
Among what might be called the poems I write

With the significant interruptions I have suffered
I cannot fully present a continuity in my life
Some things are difficult
Some hurt

And some must wait until the right time manifests itself

So!

Let us take a dig
One that may be counter to many here in the West
(Though I point out that my country Australia
Is hardly Western- more southern I would say)

This strident view if it were to be
Might challenge some at least
The initial question to be put forward
About the world scene is:
Could anyone claim the USA is not belligerent
In its attitude to many other countries

Of course we need to distinguish between
The apparent reaching out they do
Said to be humane and democratic
And the reality of their belief in their own dominance
Belligerent!
It's one way to typify the force they use to spread their thought
As well as their culture
Over the world

Another question is: does this influence penetrate everywhere
Will every gap be filled?

It can well be said their dominance
Has induced so much of Western Civilization
To unknowingly bow before them

So often the kowtow
In Europe and the Americas
And parts of Asia

One could almost feel sorry for them
That China and Russia have not yet capitulated

Does America still believe in Manifest Destiny?
In doing whatever it takes to achieve their goals?
How much of it is the condemnation of other countries
Say they're wrong and undemocratic
Or rogue states
And then continually criticize them in forums
The world over

We cannot mock them
We know the harm they do to other countries
Either in the forums
Or at times by military intervention
As well as their development and sale of more and more armaments

Rustle the cattle
Move the herd
The nations corralled finally
Leaving the way for capitalism
American capitalism

It is unfortunate for the rest of the world
We know the force of the claim of freedom
The issue of their own licence
And that means anything
Freedom to do anything

And yes we do know the harm that does

Some say cats have 9 lives

My darling boy
My cat
Is waiting
Stretched out in relaxed fashion by my chair
As I come out from the shower
Dressed at 2.30am
Yes in the morning
And he would like to come to bed with me
For our habitual snuggle
Yet I need to say
What I need to say
Bore that I am
To myself and others
As well as to him
Mister Milo
For he wants attention:
You must wait

Meanwhile he rests at my feet

*

I will ask a question
One which many may not believe to be of permanent importance
Saying that the world goes on
And we must do so with it
So the question is
Are we born into meaning
Or do only some believe this?
If we are is the early memory of those around us
Sufficient unto the purpose
A way we have of sustaining a good view of life?

Or do we
Even if happy when young
And whatever we might be called
Able adjusted sociable sensitive intelligent
A long list of words to use
Though they often cannot pin down the encounter
Between us and how we feel we lived then
And how we live now?

*

A chronology could help

It could be that a claim to be Cronus also helps

Ask of course when it is we join the Gods
And since there are so many rankings
Different generations
And among them conflict
We never fit
Being merely human

Yet as time goes by
Chronology becomes more important
Some might say lest we forget
Though I suggest it is necessary to search our individual memories
Which as we know
Exist in the midst of all around

*

1 or 2 or 3 or 4 we number onwards
Today at 75 I can look back
There is memory
There is response to others

And learning
And at times repudiation of what one sees as wrong
There are all the men and women I have known
And quite a few I have not
Seen on screen in front of me
They tell me something as I age
If I read things properly I will come
To some form of understanding

It is in this that chronology helps
Sequence and consequence over time
We all need to know something of our time
There is no way in which answers to everything
Will come to us
But we need an established sense
Of what's around us
And what could be
As well as some idea of what the future will bring
Something not yet here
In a way distant and unshaped
Yet knowing this it can only help
If we take part in what is happening today

If we let the world go to hell
That is what it will do
And whoever we are we go with it

Whatever it is that different religions and myths say
We might then have only chaos
And this can only be
A poor end to Cronus
And our own chronology

Some words

I suggest you not be profligate in your emotions
As well as advising you against believing excessively
In the rightness of the society around

Do not allow those who wish to dictate
Be they rulers parents or patrons
Do so arbitrarily
They are there assuming a position
Even perhaps one of grace
And we in our good grace
Should not allow them to dictate
Unless there is some sense in their words

How many of those ruling formulate something
And we outside their circle
See they have fooled themselves
Having spent little time or effort in the attempt
They expect followers to have faith in them
And believe in the view they take
And the work they do

So many mistakes are made
When matters are wrongly perceived
So much wrong is done
When those at the top deceive

Speak up

Speak up
Let your voice be heard
You've been silent long enough
You have no need to yell or scream
But need to be firm in your delivery
Having a real interest in what you're saying
Talk to others
We all know today
We all know
The future of the planet does not look good
We need to treat it well
When politicians get together and compromise
We cannot automatically accept the outcome
Take note
If we're not careful they may ruin us
All of us
Only our voices remain
The world has waited a long time to hear them
The voices of those kind and thoughtful
Those without ravaging minds
Essentially today we need to be good
To believe

If you are religious
And your grouping operates only on ritual
Leave it
And think again

St Kilda

Once again it happens
Up and down
This week we are defeated by Fremantle
Who are without a doubt a good side

But is there no way to arrest these bad performances?
Form obviously plays a part
Determination as well
And application to the task at hand
Is the coach lacking somehow
Nice fellow though he might be?
They approve of him
Yet he seems incapable of making any moves to save the situation
When it's failing

Once the coaches would interfere during games
And it could have some significant effect
While today they just look on
Is it the team of coaches that holds them back?
Or is it only the players
The game being played at such a pace
Hectic non-stop and exhausting?
If your game plan is working you leave it as it is
If it is not there's nothing you can do

Time after time game after game
We the supporters
The spectators
See the team being run over
Not up to the mark
Not physically strong enough it seems

Yet occasionally it all clicks
Performance improves
They all work together as a team

Whatever may be the case
As a long-time supporter
I know the game is different from what it was years ago
And the serious question crops up:
Do they fight it out?
Or are they lost in the game
Confused by its speed
And the opposition's ability?

As in so many things
You often get very close to resigning

Strangers in the house

Where or when do we start?
Though better not to
There are many alone
Many isolated
Is there reason?
Is there cause?
Is it in the house
Or only there
Outside there's life
Some say in abundance
I believe I have
Yet only in some sort of way
I know it is not always so
Has not been always so for me
Nor for many

At this stage do we ask about community?
Do we remember days of the past
Were we there
Or did we only hear
And then place them in our memory

Parents friends and partners
Where did they go?
I cannot race them or chase them
You must let them go
Yes they may come again
But where will you be
Waiting
Standing still
Or gone long ago

Has the existential angst descended again
Have I beckoned Beckett from his grave
Only heads in the sand
Signifying Watt?
Or to be still more foolish
Wanting to look again to Joyce
To juice the bastard
And like him present the domain
Not quite definite
But referring elsewhere
And people it with figures acting in front of our eyes?
We might ask where the words come from
Yet we probably care little
He told us early of epiphanies
So were we all to take up somehow
The religious mantle
The view that so much writing
Has a spiritual overlay

So do I stand outside?
Did I die with Camus when the car crashed?
The spirit gone forever

Or are we forever outside?

Those who know
Know that Heaven will not help them
Yet there are many mantras
We recite at times in our minds

I still agree with Descartes
Though many have only focussed on the one thought
There were more

To think and continue doing so helps
And although there are those who say
Weapons are powerful
There are times when thought can change the world

Stress

(1)

There is no question I feel it at the moment
To say what it's composed of
Is less easy than to lay it out

Yet over the last couple of days
I have been thinking it would be sensible
To get in touch with David
And as I said to Joan (Alannah's stepmother) this evening
David might provide a psychiatric objectivity and understanding
That would help me

Over the time of the lockdown I've seen little of him
Mostly talking through tele-health consultations
And given my lack of love of phone conversations
I would rather see him in person

Last 25th April
About 3 and a half weeks ago
He emailed wishing me Happy Birthday
Apart from that I have not seen hide nor hair of him
For 7 to 8 months

I am well aware of the increase in mental health difficulties
People have been experiencing
Over almost 3 years now
It seems there are not enough psychiatrists or psychologists
To go around
And it's doubtful if there have been sufficient
Trained over that time

To use one of the familiar words of today
I am perhaps to be typified as resilient
I have coped so far
Yet I feel I need some kind of a sounding board now
(Or at least soon)

For years I have seen psychiatrists over a 2 week period
Yet now is now
And I need some form of contact

Sometime over the last week or so
I lost my favourite jacket
Alannah and I have hunted for it
And I have gone over most of my movements
And covered the possibility of where I might have lost it

It has not turned up
And after a few days of searching
I'm resigned to the loss
Yet there is the fact behind this
And that is
I can think of no other time
When I have so blatantly and outrightly lost something
And not eventually re-discovered it

Now success seems close to impossible

So yes I do what I need to do
Resign myself to the loss
And perhaps if I can find another I like as much
Buy that
However in all this there lies beneath the surface
A serious dissatisfaction
And it is on that involved not only my jacket
But much of the world around me
I am uneasy in it at the moment

(2)

I am in the middle of an experience
As are many with political interests
And tonight (Saturday May 21st)
We might all get an indication of who will govern the country

I hardly ever predict
However I expect it to be close
And I understand if some Independents are successful
Something I do not mind
Though it seems that many of them
Though not happy at all with the ruling Coalition
Have come from backgrounds with liberal sympathies
They are not to be condemned
Yet it is interesting to note such a fact
When for quite a while in the early stages of the campaign
The Coalition wanted to personify them
As some sort of body that existed as a front for Labor

There is much deviousness in politics
And the Coalition could hardly claim
They are not prey to it

It would be good if all were good and honest
Yet it is not so
There are dirty tricks
And sometimes cranky arguments
And we (which includes me)
See the continuing putting forward of policies
By both the major Parties
And to say it fairly
They both attempt to attract voters
And the contest looks remarkably like a sale
Whoever bids the most believes they can win

I may somehow sit here as a puritan
But I am disturbed to see much of the behaviour
Yet it is a contest
And what can we expect?

With such a question in mind
I always need to step back
The only answer is
We need fair talk and behaviour
And are better without the unruly

Do not be foolish enough to believe this means
There should be no passion or compassion in politics
Nor should the participants lack conviction
But when we see duplicity we need to call it out

(3)

You might think I have no troubles
Yet I have some
Some relationships can cause me difficulties
And my writing is uneven these days
Julie who produced the only book I've done
Has failed me over the last number of years
Yet I still wish to put out at least another one
Except I want when published not to sell it
But give it away to interested people
I have no desire to be widely recognized
For me the giving avoids any money nexus
Though not everyone would agree
My sense is there is a chance
When a book comes from someone you've spoken to
And it has cost you nothing
That it is in a way (though only I may believe this)
Better than existing in merely money terms

Be assured I will not be giving away so many books
As to upset the commercial book trade
But I do not want money for what I write
I have enough to live on
As it is

Let something
Whatever it might be
Happen for me
And I will welcome it

And perhaps be happier

Talk of Dad again

But only as a starting point

Tonight I remembered when at 20
Dad did something for me
Of course he hadn't bought me a car
As he had Kent my younger brother
He had I'm as sure as can be
No understanding of the general angst he'd caused me
A man
The head of the family
Not to be relinquished to anybody
Even if the other spoke sense

So what was this attempt on Dad's part?
He had obviously spoken about me to JJ Brown
The secretary of the Railways Union
As well as the Communist Party of Australia
And JJ his old compadre through Dad
Had offered me a job as his secretary

There was a small temptation
Because of Dad and his background
I still believed in the Union movement
And its history
What it had done and what still needed doing

Yet the offer was too late
My mind was elsewhere
I was trying to understand the world's knowledge
Or more to the point what it meant to be in the world
Knowing that what was required
Was as full and fine an experience as possible

At the same time
At age 20
I had barely passed anything since Dad had forced me
Into a subordinate position
It was not just being a son
He did with his original dictates
Force me into an unnatural obedience
And hence there was a cloud forever over me
Though I did the best I could

I know our encounter forced on me a cynicism
That I had never had before
Yet I attempted at Uni as best I could
Hardly achieving academically
But trying to see what it was I needed
And a strong part of that was a cross disciplinary appreciation
The singular disciplines as they stood
Were not adequate to my needs or understanding

So you see
My mind was not with Dad
Or even fully with my past
His world was not the one I wanted
Though I understood his needs to some degree
I was searching
Searching elsewhere
Not always clear as to what
Not always clear as to why

But I did know when Dad presented the possibility
Of the job to me
It was past the time
It was part of his past

And though today I do not damn him for it
I know
That since our one argument
Our paths did not converge again for many a year

If ever

The Categorical Imperative

What am I to do?
Can I only play with the thought of Kant's categorical imperative?
When we feel things fixed in place
It can be difficult to shift them
I have some understanding of why we categorize
And most of us understand imperatives
So where is the difficulty?

The truth is it can be multi-faceted
And difficult to portray

We often wish to talk to people
In fact we often do
Yet many people friends and foes alike
Can cause trouble in a discussion
If we think and convey what we say overmuch
In any usual way
Perhaps we should try to remain flexible
We need to be aware that the other will not always be so
Does this mean they fit into a particular category
Or is the question itself too reductionist?

Yet the upbringing the education or training
And often the solidification of opinion in a particular profession
Can make life difficult for many of us
Those professing and those subject to it

We need ask:
If the above is the case
Will the conversation be satisfactory?
Are we sufficiently able to move beyond any category?
Either us or the other?

At this point I must wonder
In terms of learning there are ways which box you in
With my strong belief in cross/or/ inter-disciplinary thought
My hope is communication can take place
We need not assume strict borders
The wider the knowledge and experience one has
The hope is you can keep steady
And your life intact
It does not help being monolingual
But at least with English as your main language
Some hope remains

I know of myself
I can talk too much
So some responsibility rests on me
An active mind can be a bother to others
As well as occasionally to yourself

Nobody should be damned
When conversations go astray
We can re-engage at another time

Is it best to keep these thoughts to myself?

Perhaps so
Yet if not expressed
Others will never know

So as in a number of contexts
I remain betwixt and between

The Prime Minister's commitment

Whatever it is I feel
I cannot be sure
Either it is a great worry over me
(And it may be over all)
Or it is somehow a looseness of mind
Different from my usual state
But one where I hear
And may not even check the facts

So am I living in impressions
Reality evading me
Taking in what I see
And maybe feeling it's all too much?

I hear on the midnight news
Our Prime Minister speak
Is he telling how great he is
How well he looks after us
Or is it only bragging
A wish to impress
Saying that with the advent of AUKUS
We will soon be getting an advanced defence technology
Including hyper-sonic missiles

*

The present government has been largely going to pieces
Over the last few months
But our Scott
Admirable as he is
Zealous in his application
Now shows stronger signs
Of what he and his kind are like

The country
Our country
Is not fair and free and democratic
It is becoming essentially more militaristic

We hear what is going on
The reports are around
People such as I do not hold major or responsible
Positions in government
So there are many of us subject to these people
The hawks of the world
They hang in the air
Waiting to swoop
And what will be our end?
Though we were once citizens
We are now subject to those in control

If the hawk dives from up high
Likely we die

*

Yet given the world of today
It may not be so
Our deaths might be caused by drones
Not as natural as the hawk
This we know
But they can be as deadly

Or more so

*

[Listen to the leader
Telling us that there is a clear link
Between our economic interests and our defence industries]

As a thinker he is like many others
All over the world:
Sad people
Thinking as they do

The shifting world

What do we need to ask?

When did NATO start?
And who or what initiated it?
How has it spread?
Has its nature changed with the fall of the Wall
The Soviet Union disintegrating
Yet over a period of time Russia attempting to re-establish itself?

Ukraine lies there
Some say desperate
Some may think a spoil

Can we be in any sense sure
That those who speak for NATO
Really have Ukraine's interests at heart
Or do they just see it all
As important to an existing order
One already there
Strong in their minds
Maintaining the West
And its future?

For reasons we may never understand
Though we try
And try again
Russia is seen as alien
A pariah

It is easy and proper to call it an Imperialistic power
Its relationships to the Baltic States

And those around indicate this
Yet we must not be one-sided in our consideration
The Western powers
Especially as epitomized by the USA
Are nothing but strongly Imperialistic
In ideology and approach

Who speaks for Ukraine over the news today
Blinken the Secretary of State
Biden's man

Sometimes we
People in this world
Talk of geopolitics
So the question needs to be asked
Geography yes there's distance involved
How many miles away from Ukraine is the USA
How far away is the speaker Blinken?
How far should their reach be?
If their utterances are not indicative of Imperialism
What is?

Do we need to change the idea
Or do we need to stop and think
What was Imperialism once?
What is it now?
Is it tentacles reaching across nations
Infiltrating minds
Or is this interpretation too crude?
Do we just accept the words of the peoples of the Nation
Those who wish to be dominant in this world?

If we do this we bring the concept up to date
They are there

They have established themselves
Every effort is put into holding their position
And as we all know they believe it to be theirs by right

*

So what of self-determination for Ukraine
Is the whole idea wrong or useless
That is without value?
Will it never happen for smaller nations
Especially those that may have had little organized governance
Or been colonies or are placed in very difficult positions
Insofar as their relation to major powers might be?

*

Here in Australia we see difficulties
Ways in which our lives society and culture
Have been determined by outside forces

Today we have close to 25 million people
Yet this does not negate past dependence
And alliances with other countries
Alliances we may not consider healthy

*

We know here in Australia
Though we often say its multi-cultural
That different segments of the population
Relate to other countries in different ways
England Scotland and Ireland in the early days
But since then there have been a fair number of European states
That we relate to

And over more recent years
Some Australians have realized sensibly
The relations we can and should have
With those from South-East and Asian countries

The Vietnam War woke us up from what was
an uncomfortable situation
Yet in this our country
There are those who still majorily identify with the Western Powers
And some who see us as a bastion
For their values

Those who know Australia a little better
Know that our thoughts and allegiances
Are much wider now
Than the thoughts we had of the Mother Country
Or Anglo-celtic groupings

We can all live together
We do
But however that may be
We must understand ourselves and our region

*

This long diversion may seem of little point
Yet self-determination is an important issue for Ukraine as well
And is there any way in which they can achieve it?

Caught between the powers
There is push and pull on both sides
It is necessary to recognize that it is not only Russia
That is the Baddie

I've stated the sides
Russia is strong and aggressive true
And as the Soviet Union had a history
Of Ukraine being part of it

Yet we need also to ask
Is the USA admirable?
Is NATO something we need to understand?
Are we to believe the pressure on Ukraine
Is all from Russia
Must we not recognize the pressure from the West
(Even the enticement)
With a determination to bring the country into its sphere of influence?

I have never been to Ukraine
Nor to the USA
Yet here in Australia
I know that American influence
Economic political and cultural is strong
As well as the military reality
And it pervades our country
We know how difficult it is to be ourselves
We know of social and cultural change
Here there and everywhere
We know that some of the influence is insidious
And we should resist it

The small and the large

My little boy is not well

Only a cat you say
But is that not meaningful?
Certainly to Alannah and me

Here I am in the dining room
About to discuss something with myself
While I should be up in the study working
Transcribing something from a week or so ago
And it's true while doing this
I should be checking up if he's yet come back
To the front garden
So I can call him in
And wipe him dry after the rain there's been tonight

What is wrong with him?
Well we were told last Thursday
His hormone levels are about twice what they should be
It's a hyperthyroid problem
His energy waxes and wanes
At times I worry about his breathing
It's shallower than usual

*

I will start again and say
I am not happy for another reason
Of late I have been very much so
It's been building
The USA Russia Ukraine
China and the formation of the Quad

And I still say America is flailing
Yet it will not let go
It needs the power and position it has
And needs it recognized
We see the Presidents there over quite a number of years
Posturing themselves
I will not criticize their democracy
Though I know they need to do so
But whatever they might be
Or whoever is in charge
They need their dominance
And want it recognized
Other countries may rise in opposition
The USA then calls on its allies
Some call it International Relations
Some ingratiation
Those believed to be allies either stand by them
Or if not they are largely shunned
No country can relate to them
Unless it's on their terms

If we lived in a world where one nation was dominant
And it seemed we had no other choice
Then it could well be we would need to turn to them
Yet even now there are rising powers
And that troubles the one claiming its position
The thoughts become complicated
Things change over time
Some talk of hegemonic power
And some even when trying
Will fail to understand

Do I understand? Do I try?
There is much I don't know
Facts forgotten or disregarded

Yet the attempt is there
Look and listen
Look and see

*

I was subject to some right-wing banter today
You could hardly call it discussion
If calling it right-wing sounds wrong
Think about it
Think of how much of the world's politics
Its business its approach and its ideology
Has been determined by what are called the Western Powers
They are not immune to criticism
Though perhaps they are not a solid bloc at any one time
Yet they with their development over time
Have created large Empires
Their argument would be they've done much good

Leave that for the moment
And consider the conflict in Europe now
I do not excuse President Putin and the harm he's done
Though what I do see is almost all the Western Powers
Are against Russia
Blinken the US Secretary of State leads the charge
In his smooth and diplomatic manner
He talks of war
I should say he talked of war

For week after week the US President could only say
War is imminent
Is this diplomacy? Is it helpful?
Will these people never talk?
Or is it to be forever posturing
Unfair you might say of me

A fair distance away
And with little understanding
Yet if the people involved had some
What has happened may not have happened

The banter around me
I could hardly see as useful in understanding the situation in Europe
It was mainly just people expressing confidence in their own opinions
Without wanting to listen to me at all
So no it was not a discussion
And as such it had little worth
Rather it was a consolidation of views

It did however have some effect on me
Turning my mind to some matters that are integral
To such situations

*

People groups and crowds
What to say?
We know that we should relate to people
Whether this we is everybody I cannot say
But I believe there is an essential relationship between all people
And we need to remember this

So if the people we're involved with do as they should
Keeping in mind sensible practice
Matters should be able to be worked out

Yet when the group is large
Or too large for you
Question why you're there
Question the assumption of involvement

Approach or be in groups
With an awareness of what's going on in them
And when it is necessary judge what the group does
Know that there are some matters that are implicit
And the other members if there earlier than you
Know this

So do I suggest we leave when we have suspicions?
Yes I do

When the pervading talk is of sport
As it often is in Australia
There's no great harm in joining in
Yet when there are political matters discussed
Be a little wary
I do not suggest you be fearful of the other's thought
Yet do not allow yourself to be drawn into them
If they show narrowness or bigotry
Or if the discussion is hardly that
But really only banter
You should know by now that too much political banter is not healthy

Leave if you will
Leave if you must
Though you should not be constrained only by your own ideas
And those of your friends
Remember
Recognize
That there are many misleading thoughts in our society
And there are those who follow them too easily

Are we talking of formal or informal groups?
Both
Obviously the informal may be easier to move in and out of
Though occasionally those involved may consider you to be offensive

In doing so
However there are times when you need ask yourself
What it is you're committed to

We talk of formal groups
They differ from the informal
Being regulated in some ways
And often relating to work situations
My logic leads me to advise people
That if it's possible do not commit to work
Or working groups
If they have ideologies which may be harmful to you
Or to the planet

*

Here it is necessary to introduce Industrial Democracy
Or Participatory Democracy
While for the moment we leave the much vaunted political claims
Those that often fail us

Many workers have been duped by companies
The intentions they express to beginning workers
Often cloak facts involving their employment
And they may be obscured by the little knowledge and control
The new worker has

*

This is not an explanatory exercise
It is the laying down of a few facts

People talk of democracy
Especially in Western nations
They believe they have a good idea of what it is

And often believe that their countries are democratic
It's a proud boast
Yet the truth is that in many countries that's all it is
In many ways democracy is a fragile matter
And people need to act in certain ways to sustain it

We all know of oligarchies and meritocracies or bureaucracies
Ruling the country
Those elected to do so
May often not do the job in any sort of democratic way
Or they can be influenced by powerful lobby groups

If we consider what goes on in many countries
We realize that much political and economic activity
Is only for the good of the few
(The increasing affluent)

If democracy is to be sustained or even more
Re-established in countries
We need to keep in mind thoughts of fairness
Of social justice and equity
And have some resolve to integrate Industrial and
Participatory democracy

[As things stand at the moment
There is a long way to go]

The spirit that unites us all?

Blow the bugle
Take aim
Is it that you do whatever you choose?
Are you the leader in this country
Or are you the government
Choosing which you prefer
Commemoration celebration
Signifying something
That all Australians are supposed to know
Its meaning?

Tonight is Friday
Anzac Day is Monday
A long weekend
And Monday is my birthday
(I'll leave that thought for the moment)
What I must say
For it does not make me happy
Is the way the day
And the thoughts involved
Are spreading across the land
And now all AFL matches this weekend
Are having an Anzac Day ceremony
All 9 matches
This is 9 times more than there were once
When any significant ritual was only for
The Anzac Day match

I watched the ceremony tonight
The one we've all seen before
Yet now more elaborate
Men and women in their khaki

A bugle blowing
Are we to ask ourselves why this is so now
The Last Post
We are supposed to respond to?

The people performing some of them young
Probably cadets
With rifles
And serious faces
Showing their skill in the ritualistic handling of their weapons

Those who are aware
Know that until John Howard acted
Befriending George W Bush
And sent over our troops to fight alongside the Americans
Anzac Day had very much lost its momentum in our society
Yet Howard knew what he was doing
Allying himself to the USA
Even though the resurrection of Anzac Day
Might be thought of as a side-issue
It was there
The alliance
And the injection of a more militaristic stance in Australia
Troops to Afghanistan
Troops to Iraq
And there were those who had gone to Timor

Noble warriors some might say
Though I do not want to ridicule
We have heard evidence of what are ignoble actions
In some places
We see descriptions in the media
And we hear evidence in courts

Yet the building up of forces goes on

Yes Donald Trump had some serious thoughts
Including Defence

Were all countries involved meant to spend more on armaments?

Buy the latest weaponry
Be prepared

*

Yes Anzac Day is my birthday
Born in 1946
Very soon after the end of World War 2

The thought comes to me every year
Yet not only on the day
Often
What is the mentality behind all this?
And what is the mentality of our country
To continue the tradition in such proud fashion?

Is it what we want
A nation of warriors
Itching for conflict
As well as our spending millions more on the
War Memorial in Canberra?

Do we have no ability to let go
To ease away from the frightful reality
That is painted before us?
To live in peace with our neighbours
And relate to them

Frankly and fully
And as well when necessary help others

Without the desire to hear the sounds of war
Forever in our ears

The use of language

It is most likely that when your language is flowing
You will get it right
The flaws
Often those in response in a stutter or a mutter
Are overridden in the flow

The flow of course may not be what you think
Not a rap or stream of consciousness
Where you are carried along by your involvement
Even love of the words
Yet only too often you can cross borders
Leading to an outpouring
That can be excessive

So some control is needed
When we speak
Our hearts and minds need to be there
So we know what we say
And why we say it

Think of a world composed of public speakers
Let us assume they have not composed themselves
Yet speak as they believe
On important matters
Stringing words together
Sometimes very long words
Perhaps esoteric

We hear them now being carried along by their own momentum
Use one good word
Another quickly springs to mind
And the belief these speakers have
Is somehow they go together

This raises the question when we consider
Thousands of public speakers all pontificating at once
Are their words being wound around
Complementary to each other?

Or is the person using them
Mainly complimenting him or herself
On their cleverness?

*

Many years ago
More than 50
I understood the inadequacy of wit
Most was oppositional or colourful or used merely
In a reductionist manner
Yet its use was easy
All you needed was some ability
I could only conclude
That it was worthwhile on some occasions
But all in all the use of language
Was not greatly helped by it
Far better to be honest in speech
Attempt some truth
And without vociferous retaliation
To those calling out for it
At least be forthright in your remarks

There must be an explanation

(1)

I cannot say
I thought the house was ours
I thought the computer was equally mine
Yet when do I use it?
When do I get to it?
The truth behind all that is that
Apart from some attempt on my part
I am seriously lonely
It will not do me
Not this way
So what can I do?
Is an answer to break some ties
Or to die?
That might appear melodramatic
But I'm 76 and it seems need a major operation
While the truth is I'm hardly fit enough for it

Whoever I am
Whatever I am
I cannot just switch off
There are important relationships
Or there were
Am I to become some mute humanoid?
It sounds silly
Yet what else is a person
Who loses contact
Walks and talks and occasionally argues
Without getting anywhere?

What is the future to be?
Where is it?
I have been asking for some time
Where am I going?
And there is nobody around to talk to
To help me
Or at least respond

Yes
Cruelty your name is Ross
Alannah is still not well
And I am not without feeling for her
But there are still no answers
No-one to turn to
No-one to talk to

I worry that it may be true
The only family I have is out there
In the street somewhere or somehow
I try to tap into it sometimes
And I do so with some success

(2)

There is a question for me
One not easily answered
What use am I to myself
Of what worth to anyone?
My belief in myself
Though not entirely void
Waxes and wanes

For years I have said Know thyself
And leave it at that
It is enough that it is so
Without any foolish thought of loving yourself

To turn such into your own view of who
And how you are
Is a form of arrogance
Establishing yourself above many
This assumed love allows you position
If you take it with any seriousness
And that is unfortunate for the way you relate
To others
People and animals in this world
And the world itself

Yet with this reality
(And I am right in what I've said)
There is an underlying problem
When some people loving themselves
Those accepting the principle
Or the mantra
Believe it puts them above others
Who do not share this view

If on this earth
We might still aim for some equality
We must be careful in expressing what we want
Let us all understand we are far better
In having some understanding of ourselves
A continuing understanding
And as good as is possible
While we recognize this idea of loving ourselves
Is essentially a form of idolatry

The self
The unsubstantiated self
Will always remain that way
So it cannot be isolated
Nor any ego we would like to have

Understand our foibles and our failings
And know that we all have strengths of some sort

(3)

There is still these days
Talk of human nature
I hardly subscribe to the view
But if there is anything I do
I suggest we aim for something worthwhile
If it is nature
Let it be good nature
Approach most in this way
Without any denial of your understanding
Something which compels your consideration
For most of life's difficulties
For all around

Help is needed here there and everywhere
We cannot do it on our own
It helps when all contribute

If we have thought or studied all there is
We have at our hands
Some grip on the knowledge needed

We must not fail each other

Those in control?

There is a very unfortunate fact
About many of our leaders
Throughout the world

And it is involved in the wrong they do
It can be because they are in the role purely for their own egos
Or it could be incompetence

If they are elected leaders
There is no fool-proof way of vouching for their competence
Many people voting think little about the elections
Or are seduced by offers from politicians
With little character or integrity
The promises can
In the opinion of those who are then elected
Be easily broken

We know there are ways of keeping leaders honest
Pressuring them and holding them to their promises
The media can help in this
Though a sensible public will be aware
That often the media itself does not do its job
It can be a mouthpiece for a view
Held by those who control it
And be nothing more than propaganda

There is some form of floating consensus around
That politicians are not honest
Some people think they're not even worth having
Not worth their salt

But it helps the political reality around us
If people
Whoever they are
The rank and file of different parties
Or interest groups
Are involved in the workings of government
And its decision-making

Too much is decided by too few
To benefit whom?

The lobbyists in a parliamentary system
Can wield significant influence
It may somehow be in the balance
Good for society itself
Or it might be in a major fashion
Only good for the groups the lobbyists represent
And the politicians they deal with

*

However we typify leaders
All of us should be aware of what is done
Said to be for us of course
But of necessity questioned

Unless the public has a continuing awareness
The corruption that some talk of
(And some find)
Can happen
And the perpetrators go on fooling us

The assumption that corruption happens only in other countries
Shows a lack of insight into our own political system
We need to be watchful

Trust is important in any society
But those with large wealth and income
Have overall a greater say
Than those without
Though many like to attribute this to ability
It need not be so
There are those who accumulate at the expense of others
And it is these who have a particular potential
That not all have

Though words such as power and influence
Are not always easy to pin down in a situation
They are important in the workings of a society
And it behoves us all to recognize this

When it is evident that some have the positions
As described above
And use them merely to their own advantage
It makes any idea of a free and fair society hollow

There needs to be recognition of those who may have power
And those powerless

*

We need redress for these bad situations
Our courts should go some way towards providing this

While the watchful eye of the citizen is
If it remains alert
A significant way of properly examining the nation

To generalize

Of course we always need to ask
To what purpose?
But we know this aint so
Sometimes the generalization slips out of our mouth
Before we've had a chance to think well on it

At this point confusion can arise in a conversation
Those involved don't know where they stand
In relation to some words or phrases
Especially those that are loose or over-emphasized

We may get our backs up when any generalization does not appeal
And we sense the person who presents it
Is attempting to impose their thoughts on you

Bad luck!
The conversation may well go down the drain

*

We are often warned by others and by ourselves
Of many things
And one of these is the generalization
A warning that could easily force us to question
The very idea of them
Do we need them at all?
And should we use them?

We need here to look at applicability
As well as utility
We know they're useful
A general comment on something can be helpful

Yet we know the many areas in which they should be avoided
And could number some off on our fingers
Culture is not easy to generalize about
Many of our thoughts are astray
Different statements can diversify
Yet conversations can clarify
As does study
Though we know that general statements about different nationalities
Or people of different backgrounds
Are matters we at least need to be wary of

Could it be true that one thing needed in the enterprise
Is an attempt over time
To cultivate your intellect
No
Not a plant growing
But to be aware of the thinking you do
And how you approach the world

*

Whatever you do I suggest you do not harass others
With your general views

In our endeavours we need good grace

To start I could say

Possibly
Hardly with certainty
But some feeling that at my age
There are some facts or categories
That matter to some people
Those younger than I
And I do not feel a great need to claim
What it is these words do

For instance in beginning
I name 3
Gender race and identity
And even as a 4th
Intellect

I hardly believe I am in the race these days
Though I do talk discuss and express
Some matters important to me
As well as some of humorous or absurd reality

Age does weary me
At least a little
Physically we weaken
It's more difficult to get to our feet
And once there stay on them

I am soon to be 76 on Anzac Day 2022
The day is one I need always face
More so than the age
A day of commemoration or celebration
I do not immerse myself in either
But as Australia becomes more militaristic

The day becomes more welcome to others
Is it the legend?
Or the celebration of it that stirs people?

I have many questions surrounding the way we see war
But I have said enough for the moment

*

Our physical reality tells on us over time
There are things we do
And some we never do
Perhaps they are beyond us

When at Brighton High I was House Captain
And had some capability in sport
Today I say to people
With a wry smile
If they had had 50 metre competitions in freestyle and backstroke
At the Olympics then
I may well have won them
I was exceedingly fast
Over that distance I did not have to push myself
Yet I soon came up against a barrier
My heart was not as it should have been
I could not prolong such exertion

I did engage in different sports for years afterwards
But because of the despond I was sunk in for many a year
I did not excel

*

At Monash Uni in the 60's
My heart and mind did not stop me from engaging
In varying activities

I could not at that time come in any way to terms
With Academia
There was some intellectual activity of worth
Yet whatever the case
I did not fit the usual mould
And went my own way
My father had set me on a path of failure
And it took years before I saw my way out

(2)

Back to the beginning
(Not always the best place to be)

I could also run fast when young
Yet after Dad defeated me
With his control
I could see little point in contests
And it is still so today

Though there are some matters I write about
And strongly believe in
I will not take up the cudgels for them
My words must be enough

The contests implicit in society
Remain unresolved
Even when attempting to explain
I do not expect to win
But there is still some purpose in me
I chip away at those I do not like
Those who do wrong

*

It is no use pretending the good people in the world will win
There are no necessary conditions

But even when old you must choose a side
And it's best if it remains the one you've always tried to be on
That of goodness and truth

Today I have to say

(Though first I must mention my football team today beat an opposition
That had won 3 out of the last 5 Premierships
Also I am to see my Gastroenterologist in 2 days' time)

However I started this for a particular reason:
Mainly as a prod to myself

*

Science and technology have not been properly on my mind lately

Some time ago I tried to lay out for myself
Some thoughts and perhaps guidelines
Though of course I know I will never win
Even if I ridicule thoughts such as artificial intelligence
And warn those I know of the possible dangers
And what I in many ways see as the stupidity
Of these thoughts
Knowing that they are being developed exponentially
This means much time is being given to them
While our humanity
Something we do need to focus on
Is so often neglected
The wars go on
The bad relations between nations
And often between people

Thought and behaviour are of essential importance
Not to be restricted foolishly
But understood and worked out between people

Many machines often hand-held and minute
Seem to carry the world along these days
There are those who seem to relate more fully to the machine
Than they do to other people

It needs to be asked:

As far as people go
Are we losing ourselves?

US Presidents speak

The US President in Warsaw says of Putin
The ruler of Russia
This man cannot remain

Anyone who's read anything I've written about Ukraine
Knows I believe it should as far as possible
Have self determination
Politically socially and economically

So the reader must understand I do not support Putin
Nor Russia in its action

Yet we here in Australia
And over much of the world
Are caught in a war of words

Propaganda
Grand thoughts
Grand expressions

Biden is in Poland
Yet not long after his speech The White House says
And Blinken the Secretary of State states
The USA does not have a policy of regime change

Well we know Blinken is a good looking man
We know he's suave and diplomatic
We would also like to believe he chooses his words carefully
Yet he said they did not have a policy of regime change

There is farce in this statement
We could almost call it serious farce
Regime change?
Do we mention only a few where they have at least interfered?
Panama Grenada Iran (with CIA interference)
And Chile
Do we need to go on?
Iraq Afghanistan
What they have done over many years
Has proved the lie of the statement

We are already it seems
Caught up in some sort of war
Hot or cold
A war of words or culture

Biden quotes Pope John-Paul 2
And calls on God

Is one of them
God or Biden going to subordinate
The rest of the world to their ideas?

God ruling over us?
No thank you!
Keep away
Whether that God be American or Roman Catholic
Or somebody else's idea of what we should believe
Telling us how we should see the world

These people run their countries
They build up their armaments
Some of them they sell
Providing wealth for themselves

If they are so silly
(And what else can it be)?
(Except perhaps greed)?
Let them fight among themselves
Let them kill each other

And leave the rest of the world alone

Val and me

There is probably quite a lot I could say
Though I do not know I will
This is a start
And it involves short pieces
That I do not pretend will make a whole

(1)

I begin with a small piece written 3 months ago:

Val says I'm difficult
And contradict her
True
Why might this be so?
Well though we were friends and lovers many years ago
And have known each other a long time
Over this time we have lived our own lives
Known other people and had different experiences
Alongside the fact of our different upbringings
As well we do not see each other often these days
Would people necessarily believe their expectations
Their thoughts or ways of seeing to coincide consistently forever?

Change happens

I know what I think or believe about quite a few matters
It is not sensible to be too polite
Or merely concede to a person because he or she is a friend

That is a sure way for friends to move further apart

(2)

I believe
Very close to knowing
I have over recent years
Been somewhat harsh on Val
And also though I acknowledge her part in my past
In many ways a shared past
I have not written about it
Perhaps not giving it full recognition in my memory

There is unfairness in this
I cannot redress that by my writing
Yet I need to detail something
Or things
Perhaps
Both good and bad

Our relationship was never perfect
As none ever is
Yet we talked and went places
Had things in common
We slept together and lived together for a while

I am inclined to say that in a way
She was more loyal than I
Yet again there is no certainty

At times I let her down
At other times she disappointed me
I don't believe either of us had harmful intent
Yet people are different
And often they will do what they do

Though there can be another to think of
You finally make your own decision
And even if you do what you intend
You may often not even be sure
That it was a decision at all

We are mortal

Let not Machiavelli reign
If the ends justify the means
There is on the part of those believing this
A serious misunderstanding of the link

Once something is achieved by nefarious means
The victor is given victory
A poisoned chalice
Though he or she does not realize it
Every time a sip is taken
The wrong involved in the means resonates
And those looking on while the sip is taken
Be they courtiers or the others waiting
Sense dissatisfaction in this person
The new ruler
The King or Queen who drinks
Be it wine or water

We should be patient with those we talk to

Perhaps this is true
Most of us adhere to things we believe in
Some of which can be empathy sympathy understanding
And tolerance

Yet we know there are times of difficulty
When attempting to follow what some people are saying
And we need to base our thoughts on something
Like our belief in our own rationality
We may find that there is conflict
Between us and the other

From our point of view it's best we feel or believe
That the other has some sort of coherent view
Of whatever we're talking about
Local matters regulation politics
Or the world scene
As well as the condition of the planet
And having coherence in the view of the Universe

Of course all this could be asking too much
For yourself as well as those you talk with
But somehow in conversation there needs to be
Some agreement
Some shared basis
Even
Though it will not happen every time
An opportunity for conversation to flourish
Not false and flowing no
Not just a show
But bringing your being
Your thinking being along with you
Most of the time

Let go and you may slide
And you may not know
Go too far down the slippery slope of incoherence
And the question is obviously how you climb up again?

We can extend our criticism
Take one example
It's easily picked up
Many people believe it
So I'll mention it:
How often do we see politicians
Those who are said to be governing the nation
Waffle on with insufficient sense
When asked questions?
Are they incompetent or just caught off balance?
Certainly they would be better not to shoot off at the mouth
Better to be ruled by reason

*

I ask: Am I losing it?
My answer is always a clear no
However I am tired
So tired
Falling asleep while listening to music
Reading or watching TV
Or working on the computer

Recalling a conversation from my past
Do I hear myself ask
Is it narcolepsy?
Is it that I cannot keep awake?
And therefore my concentration is not as good as it should be
Not as good as it was once?

In this world of ongoing communication facts and data
There is much confusion
Do we blame ourselves?
Or when involved watching or listening to programs
Knowing they're not much good
Actually being an insult to our intelligence
We can so easily drift off
And lose the thread?

Yes here the nexus is broken once again
The link between the program and you

[How do we learn]?

What do politicians do?

(1)

Or perhaps it should be
What do people do?

Tonight I watched some of the debate on a commercial TV channel
It's 2 weeks to go till the Federal election
This sort of debate could be helpful and/or informative
Yet we have to question this
Some information yes
But I found the debate poorly held
For the moment I will hold back and not say anything
About its informality
(We'll leave that till later)

I do believe those questioning the leaders of our major parties
Tried in their approach
They were overall fairly respectful
Though the MC had little to say in it all
Little control
And those performing (the politicians) realized this
And took advantage of the situation

I did doze off for about 10 minutes or so
But was awake most of the time
I awoke to watch the contenders contending
Hardly respectful to each other
When one was asked a question the other cut in
Is this the political situation in our country
He (or she) with the stronger voice prevails?
Or is it that they cannot listen
Cannot allow the other to complete their presentations

Short as they are?
Is it a politics where much of what is said
Rankles the other side
So there can be only one answer?
Drown them out
Done either at such a forum
Or in the media or at the polling booths
The louder wins
The thoughtful are neglected
And possibly forgotten

There is much about all this that does not suit me
My mind is appalled at such behaviour
The nation's leaders?
Can we be sure?
Is it what we want?
Many of them are as they present:
The nation's ratbags

(2)

My heart cries out when I see them
And I can only ask why?
I feel the need to say that whether it would work or not
What we need are some informal meetings
Somehow the structure provided by parliament and the media
Social or public
Fails us
The people providing them seem to have little idea
Of the boundaries that might be necessary
So they allow a fight
A wrestle
Something that negates the possibility of decent politics

Land a blow here and there and you win

Of course I'm ignoring the audience
The people watching
They may be able to discriminate between good and bad policies
And good and bad responses
And they may have the sense to ask of themselves
Would one of these people do anything?
Be good for their country?
Be able to judge them beyond their obvious boisterousness
Or even their stumbles?

I for one have little time for these debates
For any in fact

*

I know I will not live forever
Yet what I would like to see
Like to know was happening
Would be many more informal talks on politics
And let everybody talk more fully on many topics
Including those that have been taboo for years

Let there be a greater mass of good conversation
In society
Let it build up

Many might not remember the late 60's and early 70's
But there were active minds then
(As there are now)
Yet I believe the range of thought to have been wider
And in some ways people saw a future
And there was hope in their hearts

What have we done?
Is it all of us?
Taken away from the young what they could have?
Is it me or people like me
Or is it the leaders
Many of whom are there for themselves?

Old though many of us are
We must be damned if we deny the possibilities of expectation
To the young

Is it too foolish to ask:
Could a single vote make a difference
Or a word spoken or one written
Do something for the future of us all?

What happened and why?

Have we spread ourselves too wide?
Has the knowledge we once had
And possibly understood
With some control over its use
Splintered irredeemably across the world?

The penchant among many for trivia
Point after point
Question after question
Often of ridiculous randomness
We need to ask
What value does it have?
What really needs to be asked?

Or more fairly said
Talk among yourselves of the putting together of knowledge
General knowledge maybe
But certainly in various areas
Areas specific to us as humans
People dwelling upon the planet
With a huge range of insects animals and fish around us
We need to care for

As well as many other problems

Of what use is it to only act in a trivial fashion?

What is our country worth?

I can't say that Australia is not still
A man's country
I have been waiting
If that's what I'm doing
For many years
And a lot has not changed

The nation we are told to be so proud of

Are we only people engaged in sport
Or the military?

All across the world more money is being put into Defence
And we let the leaders do it
Voting them back time and again
And while this happens
The parties in opposition
Most of them
Those we might look to and expect to moderate support
For the rifle the gun and the tank
Do little in the role they should play
Hardly speaking up against a national pride or hubris
On the part of many in high positions

Spend more money on the War Memorial in Canberra?

How do we divide the thoughts of Nationalism and tourism?
Much is in the name of commerce
And its intention is a further glorification of the country

There has been over the last 2 weeks a program on 4 Corners
The ghosts of Timor

Some in the country may have watched it
And some understood

The first overseas assignment for Australia in the United Nations
It was said at the time to have gone well
Yet did it?
4 Corners reports bad practice even torture
On the part of the SAS
And towards the end of the program
The question asked is
Did what happened in Timor
Set a precedent for the bad behaviour we have read of
Day after day in the newspapers
Here in Melbourne?

I am tired so tired to hear
When the next Governor-General is announced
That more than likely it will be a military man

This is our country
Do these people represent us?

I would not salute them
Nor take their orders

Let there be here
For our sake
The appointment of people from other walks of life

But though I generalize
Let not the alternative be the likely one
Members of another cult we have
The supporting cult

Yes participate
Play sport and be healthy
But once again do not glorify the thought

The truth is I think it best not to glorify anyone
What I would do more often than the authorities do now
Is choose governors and their like
From many groupings

So we have the possibility of relating
To many more people in society than we do

What's happening all over the world?

Stan Grant
On Insiders Sunday morning
A person whom many may know
Indigenous an Elder quite learned in many areas
Including foreign affairs

He says Australia's Defence spending
Must go up from what it is now
Given the state of the world
The uncertainty
1 and a half to 2 at least and probably 3%

He says this as a responsible commentator
Indicating Australia is under threat

But to what extent and how has it changed?
He emphasizes the threat of China
And sees a Russia/China nexus of sorts
Does he explain this fully?
In any complete way?
Hardly:
He's presenting a viewpoint that fits in with those who worry
And constantly think of war
And the threat from other countries
And in all this what do we (Australia) need:
Strategic allies

Can that ever be the solution?

The Insiders is a political program on the ABC
There is a guest in the middle of the program
And a MC throughout
As well as three journalists who have varying levels of expertise

There is quite a lot to talk about
Australia not doing well with the floods in Qld and NSW
And many think the Federal government is not handling things well

Eventually we come to another crucial issue
That of war
And from the beginning of this conversation
Stan is a major voice
Stan Grant

He speaks with authority
There seems to be little possibility
Of any in the group
Being a voice for peace

Many know Vladimir Putin started a war in Ukraine
It could be a mad solo performance
Or it could in some way succeed
No-one wants to see force prevail
Nor the suffering in Ukraine

Yet for some time the West and its allies
Have been talking things up
The drums are beating so they say
And so many of them feel confident in their predictions
War will come
We must prepare
And of course in the eventuality it finally does not
We will end up stronger and more fortified

Step back a little
Ask what we're seeing
And what we've seen

In the past the Hawks had their way
They built up their arguments
They built up their armaments
They told us there were enemies out there
Enemies to be defeated

I know if we isolate countries
They will feel isolated

I know that many of these people
(Often the commentators)
Though said to be experts on the world scene
Seem to have a desire for conflict
Is it to prove their dominance?
Could they be as unsure as we are?
Is that why they step back
Or hold off?

In this world
With many nations having nuclear weapons
It is only good sense to talk
To talk or negotiate
And try to move towards some peaceful reconciliation
Keeping the world alive

When do we know if it is so?

We watch and listen
And when we know we must we ask
Are these people in public office hiding behind masks
Pretending to be something other than they are?
Or do they have some honesty in approach
Are all politicians not bad or useless
Are they capable of running the country
Both sides
All sides
Or will they ruin it?

We would be foolish to believe them all to be raving fools
Yet we need to ask of many
How did you get where you are
Was it by a forthright approach to the people
And problems perceived
Or by deceit
One held to in your term of office?

Can we trust you?
Or is it only that we must?

Are there those who can only be called ruthless
Able to climb to the top?
How many bodies?
How many lies?

It is familial
Even within a medium-sized country
The coterie might agree with you

When there were Kings and Queens
The courtiers courted
The aristocracy deferred
Generally
Though if not they had to calculate the odds
And could lose their heads if too extreme
Or else if their approach was less so
Some of their estates could go
And their power be diminished

We are not foolish enough here in Australia
To see the Prime Minister
As the King is seen
His power depends on a variety of things
Personal ability
Factional support and loyalty
An ability to mediate between his Ministers

The PM does not always command overtly
Yet we know he or she is there

I suggest you do not lie
Or mislead Parliament
Nor should you mislead the people
They deserve respect from you
Not your extolling yourself or your ability

*

Do Labor Party members today
See the world mainly in terms
Of Party politics and factionalism?

There seems evident
An unfortunate neglect of some things

And especially an important strength
Labor tradition
Is the parting word the only recognition
Mentioning Unity or Solidarity as you sign off in your email?

And it needs also to be asked
Does the Party want you and your participation
Or is it money it wants for its running
And your hands to vote

There can be needs that outgrow real loyalty
As well as belittling serious thinking

*

About a week ago
Peter Dutton a Queenslander
Was elected leader of the Liberal Party
I have no doubt this choice is contentious
I mention a female journalist in The Age
Who is overall saying give him a fair go
We need to wait and see
Knowing that many in the public have not taken to him
Over his time in Parliament
She is making some sort of case
For the possibility of his improvement
Now he is the Leader

We all know time goes past
And much is forgotten
Yet this gentleman has been in parliament for 20 years or so
And has shown unfortunate traits and some bigotry
Against different people

According to a statement of his a few years ago
Victorians could not sleep safely in their beds
Because of the threat of Sudanese youths
From the Western suburbs of Melbourne
A blatantly political and thoughtless comment
If not rabble-rousing
Words initiated by his dislike of the Labor Premier of Victoria
Loose thinking
Loose talk
Or talk to a purpose?
A man involved in national security
No friend to refugees
There can be in such people
Suspicion of the Other
And his thought and behaviour
At times illustrate this

I do not believe Jacqueline Maley
The journalist I mentioned
Believed there would be a marvellous change in Dutton
So what did she believe?
Was it only a journalist saying
Give the new leader a go
Do not pre-judge him?

However what is missing here is important
The taking seriously of the unfortunate things he's said and done
In his 20 years in the House of Representatives

If all journalists were to write their pieces on any politician
Only outlining political faults of the past
Without expressing some form of judgement
It would be hardly worth reading them

When I am myself and when not

As yet I'm not desperate
But there grows upon me a feeling
(Is it a knowledge)?
An identification with the outcasts
The outsiders
Taking up again without the wish of doing so
The way I was when young
The lost relationships partly
But something else
Assuming again an identity perhaps
One of dissatisfaction and unhappiness

I wrote a piece lately on chaos
And attempted to explain it
Implicit was a sense of relationship I had
Years ago

An age of youth
An age of cynicism
Even if people could not tell you knew
You no longer believed
Faith gone
At this time there was the strong sense of being cast out
From the family circle
What had been a comfort was now a strain
This new being whatever it was
Had to look elsewhere
The love and consolation of home was no more

I look back all those years and ask
Was I so easily defeated
Made redundant among the group

Any group
Only able to make contact in single fashion
And then still unsure
Some solace sure
In the arms of some
Or the words of others

It is then I started writing
Good bad or indifferent what matter!
Some outlet some expression
Words were hard to come by then
I did not know what was needed to produce
But I achieved a few things

For quite a number of years I was not at ease
And living out my late youth was difficult
There was serious restriction around my mind
Dad's bonds cut deep
So many things I had wanted to do
And so little done
Yet I understood the need for safety

*

An amorphous mass
Perhaps
A precise mind though wide-ranging was lost
How could this be so
I understood sequence
Attempted to understand consequence
Yet more often than not sequence was broken
And many details lost
Those I had cherished in some way

Is the cynic without form
Or only reduced in form?
Not being able to allow any creative force to break though
Restraint is dominant
And I know now as I knew then
That this restraint is not good

*

Refer to today
60 years after
Mum and Dad gone
My brothers living away for many years
Much has gone on over the time

It is obvious why I write this
Sean's funeral has had to be postponed
Simon Mara Alannah
Their family now
Whatever the mix
For most of the time take up the study

So it happens
I cannot (except at times)
Be cranky with them
But once again what I do
My own life
Its sequence
Goes by the board

And I ask myself what is the consequence?
I can handle it for a while
But only that
Whatever others think I will never again agree
To wearing blinkers as I move around

I am not a harsh and foolish fellow
But there comes a time when we all need freedom
Freedom to think and do
And as we grow older
We need even more to seek it out

Where to start?

(1)

There are options available for our attempt to understand
It could be suggested at the beginning
Historical encounters and competition
Or it could be the rivalry as it grew
Between the free world as some would call it
And the others
Though we know there is the eternal difficulty
Best described as the necessity of acknowledging
And understanding the other

I will for the moment suggest something
Though it is in no way an answer
Just a proposition
Or if you like call it a question:
Is the West
And primarily the USA punishing Russia
For being Russia?
The point could be made that there is bias in this question
Yet does asking help us to understand the unfortunate situation
We have today

As far back as the Revolution in Russia
There was opposition by the Western Powers
The British mainly composed the armies
Fighting the Bolsheviks on Soviet soil
Yet ideologically the USA had developed
Their thoughts of Manifest Destiny
While around that time there were the Robber Barons
All of which coalesced as a strong strain of Individualism

In America
They pushed industrialization further than many countries
And at the same time de-humanized or alienated
Workers in factories
There was of course a trade-off
More goods were available and often at cheaper prices
Because of the pre-dominant mass production

*

Before the 1940's
There was considerable conflict between
Capitalist and Communist countries
It might have appeared that World War 2 healed this
But overall it was only pasting over the cracks
After the War and the build-up of the military power of each
Including nuclear ability
There was what Churchill called
The Iron Curtain
And they were facing on either side

One can cover the history through to the fall of the Berlin Wall
In 1989
As well as seeing a disintegration of sorts of the Soviet Union
After this time

I will not deal with times beyond this
But at least note
How the USA in many ways gloated
Over what they saw as their victory

There is little doubt that the West
Epitomized by the US believed they could turn all the countries
Of the old Soviet Union
Towards their way of thinking

Here we need to question

But before we do we need to ask
Is the capitalist system and the freedom
That America believes it embodies
Some kind of pure thought
A fully worked out way to live?

I have more than a suspicion
That many Americans believe it is
That no other way is possible

When Communism was stronger
There was much proselytization
We know that
And over the years we saw the flaws
Yet in the USA there remains a myth
Created by many of those in power
That if left to itself capitalism will prevail

This is the point where we need to state
The divisions in the West
Race ethnicity
And of great importance the almost complete inequality
And inequity between peoples
There are many poor
Many exploited
Many given little consideration

Yet much of this is hidden
Behind a mask the West wears
The ruling elite believe in their system
Though many people have little access to it

Media accounts can distort
Those who believe themselves to be good
Are not always so
And we need to ask
Are their enemies as wrong-headed as is claimed?

(2)

As far as I can remember
I believe as long as I've been conscious
I've been against war
Spoken about it often
And over recent years written

The Russian invasion of Ukraine appals me
And I see little or no excuse for Vladimir Putin for doing so
Yet forever there is the question of text and context
We know the text and can only cry out at its happening
However the context is not simple
And must include the Western Powers
There is my belief that the USA wants
And has wanted to for a long time
Punish Russia for reasons other than the obvious
It would be good
We would all be healthy and free in our lives
If we took a one-sided view of the world
And believed America to be the peace-maker
The driving force
And though we know nothing is perfect
They believe themselves to be as close as possible

A force such as theirs can be captivating to some
Helping them to believe where salvation lies

Yet how much harm has the country done?
Today it is being said Russia will (or might be)
Using chemical weapons
And committing war crimes
Yet how many times have the USA done so
With their military
Their CIA
And as well as forcing regime change in some countries
There is the history of chemical weapons
In Laos and Vietnam
And dare we ask of them
What is napalm other than a weapon of chemical warfare?

I am not trying to balance the ledger
Putin's act was violent
I would say thoughtless
Though with my little knowledge of him
He would almost certainly have worked out a strategy

Today it appears a wrong calculation
And he must bear the weight of his wrong-doing

While his actions have perpetrated the war
What he has done has allowed a lot of loose language
Around the world
To talk of a 3rd World War
To call everyone to arms for Ukraine
Is something that could propel us further

If we wish the world to survive
The crisis in Ukraine must be resolved

(And at the same time global warming
Needs to be tackled seriously)

I do not want to say this:
But if humankind destroys itself
It will deserve to

Let leaders
And all others take note

Why oh why?

(1)

In many ways it could be good
To get away from politics for a while
They can be distressing
Can cause you anguish
And as you watch the leaders act
The leaders so-called of this world
You can feel even more seriously distressed

Why Nancy?
Nancy Pelosi
Did you make up your mind to go to Taiwan?
Was there a need?
A good reason
Or was it how you saw the world?

Of course it needs to be questioned
Do you know that you should not antagonize people
Do you know that it may be so
That despite your assumptions
The USA might not be the best country in the world?

Do you realize there are many in this world
Who do not see you as a real democracy?
We all know of the disparity of wealth and income
You have over there

Do you expect us
Whoever we are to admire you?

The fact
I feel exists fully in the need to look at yourselves
Not just believe the image you have of yourselves
But really notice the context in which you act
The harm done
The countries ravaged by your war machines
And the way you as an Empire perform
Your tentacles reaching out across the world

China is not without fault in its actions
Yes I know that
Yet you both need to be aware of the problems you cause
To other nations

Question yourselves:
Is your diplomacy and aid friendly?
Is it properly fortified by good intentions
Or are these intentions selfish
Only for the purpose of spreading influence
Spreading your culture as far as you can

(2)

I must admit I have read little of Nancy's going there
I do know her position in the USA
And have seen her speak in the past
And 2 days ago saw her masked
In the Chamber of Deputies in Taipei

If I were to follow the reasons for her going
I might be somewhat the wiser

But would it change my opinion about her going?

Though I am not she
Neither a leader politician nor ambassador
Nor am I American
It is still possible to have a view of goings-on

And I know as I see the situation
That if I were her I would not go
And the reason is simple
Firstly I need to ask if she's really standing up for anything
Or is it only the mythology the USA concocts?
And secondly a good reason a sensible one
For not going
Not taking this action
Is to not rile
Seriously rile
Another nation

Is America poking the bear again?

40 Minutes

(1)

Let us say I have little more than an hour
Can I solve the problems?
It's unlikely
Given that even the stating of them is difficult

Religion here there and everywhere
I know where I stand
And am also aware that in many ways
I still hold to the thoughts of my youth
They were:
Most of the problems would be solved
That is the initial ones
If people were to get over the hurdle of belief
Of their faith in some God or whatever they might conceive of
I thought when young
We could then all with clear minds
Approach our lives and those of others
Without this God impediment hanging over us

It might well be a new reality
Though I had no desire to name it
I thought of people coming out of the cave
Coming out from underneath certain thoughts
And working out what they would do
And this would involve what it is they thought they should do
One obvious question would be
If there is no God or gods
(And we would by then know there were not)
How could humanity fully realize itself?

I admit at this early age
I had thoughts about the good that could be done
As well as sharing
Co-operation would not be a dirty word
(I did question the thought of competition
But I'll leave that for the moment)

(2)

I watched a film this afternoon
And I realized there were a number of American films available
That talked of God
Yet they did not overdo it

This interested me
I know if there were a great number of these films
That would be over-doing it
So I felt unwilling to see more

The question is there
And it's obvious
Is this God these people talk and think about
Good or bad for the country?
And I must admit this is not a question easy to answer

There are those in different societies
Who in some way rule
Or direct their countries in certain ways
Having a belief in their God
And here's the rub
Not understanding there are quite a number of us
Who do not think as they do

So the above thought divides people
And countries
Yet I have had friends who are Christians

And we have got along well over the years
And it is not only Christians
There are many other ways of seeing the world
If you like God
(Or even the gods)

Yet I do not damn those who live in God's shadow
Perhaps they need the certainty
Or the shade

*

I could at this point say
As long as they are good people
In my eyes
We can get along
Yet there are provisos
Matters needed to be mentioned
About different religions
And one major is the knowledge of missionaries in different countries
Believing they hold the word of God in their hands:
The Bible
And these people have gone and still go overseas
To spread the word

Some would say there is no or little harm in this
Yet I am concerned
(Though I say again if some good comes of it
I must recognize it)
So why concerned?
We need all ask this
And one answer is the indication it gives
Of Christian missionaries believing they know Truth
That their ideology is the only one
And the way to live

The missionaries may have love in their hearts
Or they may have something else
They may have a mighty pride in their own religion
And their own culture

So it is necessary to ask:
Is their mission actually predicated
On a disdain for these people in distant lands
And other cultures
And not love at all?

*

I will leave this here for the moment
I am not undecided about what I'm saying
Yet I need to retreat for some little while
Not wishing to attack too strongly

My attempt is to understand what goes on in the world
And I can only suggest to any others
Attempting the same
That anger helps little
A cool appraisal is necessary

1979 again

Let us say I'm back there
Yet I started at the opposite end
Instead of Mum and her brother Mick
And Gran coming out here after World War 1
Consider if they had stayed in England

Over here Mum always said
She had no sense of nostalgia for England
Living as she did happily in Australia

But what if I
And perhaps my 2 brothers had been born in England
Our father would not be he whom we recognize today
There is no use in conjecture of this kind
But it would have been very different
Being born as I was in 1946
Just after the 2nd World War
And growing up not in Australia but over there

I do not say I regret my life
Dad's attempts to bend me to his will
Were not at all welcome
But Australia is at the least
Not a bad place
Though I often find there is much that needs to be done
Is it some form of complacency or lassitude
We experience here?
Have we still not established ourselves?
Many are satisfied
Yet there seems to have been a lost imagination
Or one never found
Transplanted people here
Adapting to a land they do not fully understand or appreciate

Brought up in Britain?
A place we here in Australia
Were often referred to over the many years of my life
When you go back
And I did first in 1979 at the age of 33
There is a familiarity
There is a relationship to the people
And the culture
Yet still on the first trip you are an outlander
London is central of course
And you can travel
If in my counterfactual world
I lived there in my early life
I would be close to the European continent
Another recognizable culture
I could have done the Grand Tour there
And followed the trails of history
Leading where?
Perhaps I have wondered about these trails for years
Wandering in my mind
Something that could have caused my disturbance
When I did go in 79
Not living in the country
Not living in the culture till then
I lapped it up
Was it all too much?
Had I read too many books from the Old country
The Mother Country
Or whatever part of Britain
England Scotland Wales
The Islands of the Hebrides
I kept reading while over there
So should I have been born over there?

Am I lost here
And undecided?
Perplexed in nature?
A nature which I have some idea of
Some feeling for
But one that has never been completely with me

The villages towns and cities
The rivers plains and valleys
The woods and mountains
In Europe
Remain in my mind
Could it be that I was born there
And was only over time transplanted to this colony
The New World and its promise?

What did I believe when young?
What was it I was seeking?
Was it here or over there?

(Did the hope of coalescence come
With the acceptance of the Orient Africa and the Americas
The desire to know the world around)?

*

What is near to our heart?
Or our mind beholden to?

(1)

Is all life petty?
Is mine of no consequence?
How is it I ask the question?
Am I the only one to do so?
Or the only one still alive?

At 15 at the time of enveloping depression
With by that time no meaning
Except in me still
There was perhaps a sense of resistance
Against who or what I cannot be sure
But my father certainly
Not Mum
Whom I loved

I know that at that age
After Dad did not listen
I wrote a little
And one phrase sticks in my mind
A mind young and possibly very narrow:
Nobody justifies their existence

Yes I know we would have to situate
The people we deny any form of authenticity
Yet I lacked a certain sophistication
At that time
Understanding the world more than I did then
And gaining experience over the years I've lived
I know there are some
Of whom I'd say
That in some way
They do justify their existence

My comment may put too great a weight on people
In an attempt to evaluate them
To judge their worth
And today I know that what I said at that time
Was an attempt to find out what mattered in peoples' lives
Were there ways of living that would make me feel more positive
Towards them?

Now
Since the world has opened up to me
And I have some meaning
Many more would find I spoke well of them
And accepted them
Though it must be said that it would be my view
And might appear arbitrary
Especially as in what might be called any pantheon
There are many people the world believes to be worthwhile
Whom I might raise doubts about

I can only define the necessary condition
As that of being good
There are those who are not so
While many of those who are
Are hardly recognized as worthwhile in this world

Yet if I can say a person is good
He or she has value in my eyes
And there is hope that in the meeting
Other qualities are part
Truth and responsiveness
Affection without pretence
And an attempt to be fair to all around

(2)

A month or so ago I used a title
Some believe cats have 9 lives
Not claiming it for myself
But now I ask
How many lives do we lead?

I have always believed in consistency
And accumulation of understanding
But when I am fully aware
That is when I allow myself to be
A fuller comprehension of what I've lived through surfaces

No numerology for me
Though John Nash believed in it and utilized it
Almost certainly needing to

The un-mathematical nature of numerology
Causes me to baulk at the thought
Numbers as we know are exceedingly important
And much can be done through and with them
But the significance that lies in numbers
Has at times to do with measurement
And precision
They also relate to people in terms of the ways
We slice up time
Naming a particular year
Or having a birthday
Or there being a special day
You would of course need to know its date
But the number itself is not significant
What is important is not intrinsic to it
But it is a basic fact
That a particular thing in our lives can happen on a particular day
At a particular time

Yet we cannot rule out any idea of intrinsic interest
When exploring numbers
There are combinations and permutations as well as series
The remarkable interest of prime numbers
As well as how to use all these numbers
The large and the small
Some might approach the infinite
Some are infinitesimal

What we need do is distinguish between working with numbers
Using them
And looking for signs in them
An area that can become largely a psychiatric matter
And a difficulty to many

(There is the important relationship in thought and language
Between the concrete and the abstract
I leave this for another time
Though with the necessity of pointing out
That it is here that many people can be subject to delusory thought)

(3)

Now before the hiatus with my father
Before the age of 15 it was quite often said of me
That I was a genius
An odd word
Rather complimentary
Yet you would be a fool to accept it
To believe it to be true
There are billions of people in the world
We relate to some of them

It is possible you might stand out in some way
Having perhaps exemplary features in some areas
Yet the word genius is like many others

Easily said
And often without much thought
It may of course be some sort of appraisal of particular abilities
Or insight
But there is one thing I know:
It is best not to label the young thus
It's usually worth little more than the name-calling people do
When young

*

So being at times called genius did not do
A great deal for me
Except to occasionally elicit a slight smile
(What do you say to such a comment
If anything)?

We all know that it is possible to fall from a great height
And seriously damage your head
And it can be so that you are no longer the same
After the fall
Being greatly reduced in many aspects of life
This includes intellectual and physical
As well as emotional
And it hurts
The experience hurts

Dad with his forceful intrusion into my life's intentions
Intervened in a way he could never understand
And thereafter there was a certain desperation in me
I held on for years
Coped as I could
But scaled no heights either physically or metaphorically
Those around did I believe
Think they knew me
Yet somehow I was not there as I had been when young

Dad and my heart operation
At age 15 and 16
Difficult to come back from

And the question always on my mind at that time:
Where was I going?

After some years of failure after failure
I finally went to University
Something that had meant something to me

Perhaps an achievement
Perhaps my mind would open again

Yet no my life since my mid-teens
Had been set on a path
And I had difficulty reconciling it
With my dreams of youth

About the Author

In my late teens and early 20's I wrote quite a lot, and even a little ambitiously.

At age 26 I had a serious breakdown, having had in earlier years troubles with my father.

I could say: who knows the cause? But will not.

I leave it at that, except to say, I had for quite a few years psychiatric problems.

However for years now I've been quite well. And though not as physically able as when I was young, doing much of what I intended doing then: writing about the world, politics, society, and anything that came to mind, as well as personal history and local matters.

It is possible to get upset by the world at times.

Yet overall it is best to try to understand and place matters in some form of historical context.

I suggest those whose concerns are, in their minds, something like mine, put them down.

The expression can only help
But let it not be raging and angry at everything
That can only be destructive.

So do as I do:
          Keep trying

www.ingramcontent.com/pod-product-compliance
Lightning Source LLC
Chambersburg PA
CBHW070649120526
44590CB00013BA/890